REBOOTING YOUR BRAIN

DAVID NAYLOR

REBOOTING
YOUR BRAIN

USING MOTIVATIONAL INTELLIGENCE TO
ADJUST YOUR MINDSET, REACH YOUR GOALS,
AND REALIZE UNLIMITED SUCCESS

WILEY

Published by John Wiley & Sons, Inc., Hoboken, New Jersey.
Published simultaneously in Canada.

For general information on our other products and services or for technical support, please contact
our Customer Care Department within the United States at (800) 762-2974, outside the United
States at (317) 572-3993 or fax (317) 572-4002.

Wiley also publishes its books in a variety of electronic formats. Some content that appears in print
may not be available in electronic formats. For more information about Wiley products, visit our web
site at www.wiley.com.

Library of Congress Cataloging-in-Publication Data is Available:

ISBN: 9781394157853 (Cloth)
ISBN: 9781394157860 (ePub)
ISBN: 9781394157877 (ePDF)

Cover Design: Wiley
Cover Image: © Line drawing of brain © Drypsiak / Getty Images

SKY10049821_062323

I would like to dedicate this book to Benjamin and Catherine. Before you were born, a friend told me, "You never understand your capacity to love until you have a child." On the day each of you were born, as I looked down into your bright eyes, I remembered those words and could attest to how true they are. As you both have grown, I've wanted nothing more than the best for you. I've wanted you to be happy and fulfilled. I've wanted you to experience everything that life had to offer. I've wanted you to love, laugh, and feel joy that seems like it will overwhelm your heart.

I hope that the words in this book will help you in your life journey.

All my love,

Dad

CONTENTS

PREFACE

Can you really reboot your brain?

Can you really let go of years of negative thinking, self-limiting beliefs, and emotional baggage?

Can you really shift your mindset and change your perspective so profoundly that you can finally achieve everything you want for your life?

If you had asked me these questions on November 1, 2021, I would have unequivocally said no. Sure, years of therapy might help to sand down some of the psychological rough edges, but it can't create a wholesale shift in a person's awareness. I would have bet a million dollars that it was impossible to reboot our brain. No way, not happening.

Then, it happened to me. I couldn't deny it. I couldn't doubt it anymore. I was living proof you could reboot your brain and, with it, profoundly change your life in incredibly positive ways.

David Naylor

PART 1

When Everything Changed

CHAPTER 1

My Reboot

On November 11, 2021, I was diagnosed with COVID-19. At first it was like a mild cold, and then I experienced increasing fatigue until it got hard to will myself to move. By November 15, I knew the virus was attacking my lungs as breathing was getting more difficult. Still, I felt it would work its way through my system and I would be fine. On Sunday, November 21, my wife, Michelle, recognized that things had progressed and not in a good way. (Candidly, she saved my life on that day.)

She took me to a local urgent care facility; I was their first patient, standing by the door when they opened for the morning. They took me to an exam room where a doctor checked the oxygen saturation in my blood and told me I was suffering from acute hypoxic respiratory failure. Basically, my lung function was so low that it was starving my cells, organs, and brain of oxygen; as a result, they were beginning to shut down and die. Without medical intervention, I would have been lucky to survive the day.

Within five minutes they had me in the back of an ambulance and were rushing me to the hospital. Little did I know that I was about to start the most harrowing, overwhelming, and frightening process of my life.

For the next five days, machines helped me to breathe while I laid in a bed attached to electrodes, IV lines, and monitoring equipment. On my third day in the hospital, despite the medical team's best efforts, things had not improved. I was being given the highest level of oxygen they could give short of being on a ventilator and still my lungs refused to accept it. Decisions were being made about moving me into intensive care from the COVID floor I was currently on. It was a dark day.

Then something miraculous happened; it was as though I could feel my family and friends praying for me. I could sense all these people sending positive thoughts and best wishes my way. By midday, my lung function began to improve. The doctors couldn't explain the sudden shift or why my lungs began to allow oxygen in. Two days later I was in a wheelchair being wheeled out to my wife's car to head home.

As I was leaving the hospital, the doctors explained that recovery would be like a rollercoaster ride in the dark. There would be no way of knowing what would come next.

As I write this, I have been out of the hospital for three weeks. I've had good days and tough days, but the ratio is moving more and more in favor of the good days. I can feel the inflammation in my lungs declining and my breathing becoming less labored. With this my energy level is slowly coming back. I am also learning to pace myself better.

It was the 19th-century German philosopher Friedrich Nietzsche who first said, "What doesn't kill you makes you stronger." Right now, I'm weaker, more out of breath, heavily fatigued, and 23 pounds lighter. I'm still holding out hope for the physically stronger part, though.

On the mental side, it has been an entirely different story. A few days after coming home from the hospital, I recognized a dramatic shift in my thought process. With this shift came the most profound positive insights regarding my mindset and psychology I have ever experienced. It was as though my brain rebooted itself. Never would I have thought that possible; then I experienced it, and I couldn't deny it. My broken brain, encumbered by fears, self-doubts, negative thinking, and limiting beliefs, had repaired itself. Suddenly, everything looked different.

My Broken Brain

Prior to being hospitalized with COVID, to the outside world it looked like I had it all together. I was the cofounder of a Top 20 Global Leadership Development company. Over the course of three decades, we had built the company from a small regional startup to an organization that did business in more than 95 countries and counted a large percentage of Fortune 1000 companies as clients.

All of this had afforded my family and me a nice lifestyle. We lived in a big house and were able to escape to our lake house in warm summer months. We took nice trips and were able to see and do cool things. I was able to afford many of the things society tells us we should own if we are successful.

To support all of this, I had built this alter ego, a second version of myself, who stood up in front of thousands of people each year and doled out wisdom and insights on how to become a better version of themselves. I wrote articles and was quoted in top magazines. I cohosted a podcast and interviewed successful people and those who had overcome incredible obstacles. I shot videos and hosted live and virtual conferences attended by people from around the world.

By most outward appearances, I was living the dream. But much was an illusion.

Inside, in the dark recesses of my mind, I was broken. The reality was profoundly different than the illusion.

Growing up, I was physically and emotionally abused. I was terrorized by a person who was themselves broken. I lived in constant fear about what would set them off. Would I be chased as they tried to catch me? Would I be struck by a belt or a hand? Or would I be lucky and just suffer from the emotional abuse of being yelled at and told of my constant failings?

Every day I tried to please, to show that I was good enough, to make them proud. I thought if I could just do this, maybe the anger would subside, and they would love me. As crazy as it sounds, this behavior didn't go away as I grew into adulthood. I still sought external validation, approval, and love from those around me, because I didn't feel good enough on the inside.

My brokenness caused me to retreat into myself at an early age; as a child I became very shy and introverted. The fear that lived within me manifested into a reluctance to try things, a constant questioning and criticizing of myself, and an overriding desire to avoid making a mistake or risk being rejected and made fun of by the "cool" kids. As a defense mechanism, I became close-minded to any opinions other than my own and rebelled against authority.

As a young teenager, I was so overwhelmingly lonely and unhappy that I consciously looked to reinvent myself. I studied the cool and popular kids, making note of how they dressed, acted, and spoke. I tried to model that behavior and work my way into the group of more popular kids. I think this was the birth of my alter ego, my second self.

Even though I was pretending I had it all together my brokenness was still there, just beneath the surface. When I was quiet and still or faced with the prospect of doing something new, it would show up in my never-ending string of negative thoughts and self-doubts. For everything I was doing to show the outside world that I was okay, in control, and put together, the voice in my head kept telling me I was a fraud and was about to be discovered as such.

As I got older, I became better at presenting my alter ego, my pretend self, to the world. I also found ways to temporarily make myself feel better and distract myself from the negativity of my brokenness.

I discovered that drinking too much could help me temporarily forget. Eating too much also made me temporarily feel better. Candy and the accompanying sugar buzz lifted my spirits, so I couldn't walk by a bag of candy without eating at least half of it.

Shopping also became a vice that temporarily allowed me to feel better. I bought a lot of things, big and small, and the Amazon truck delivered to our house every day. This is but a short list of the many vices and coping mechanisms I used to mask my brokenness and attempt to feel better. The ironic thing is, I chased all these vices and sought the short-term comfort and distraction they could bring completely subconsciously. I had no awareness or understanding as to why I was doing what I was doing; I just did it.

Ultimately, though, no vice or coping mechanism could fix me. They were like a sugar high that made me feel better in the moment, but I would always crash, and the negatively of my brokenness would come right back.

Sadly, my brokenness didn't just negatively affect me; it had a destructive impact on all those around me. My broken brain caused me to act and react in ways that undermined the quality of my relationships, pushing the people I love away, and fostering emotional baggage in their minds.

My brokenness radiated out of me and perpetuated brokenness in others. My brokenness multiplied and broke the people I care about. This is the destructive nature of broken brains.

Then It All Changed

When my brain rebooted itself, as it came back online, every negative thought and self-limiting belief and all my brokenness had been erased. My ever-present sense of fear dissolved, and I was able to feel its incredible weight lift off my shoulders. For the first time in my life, I felt whole, complete, and good enough.

I began to see myself, everyone around me, and everything around me from an entirely different perspective. I couldn't explain why, and candidly, I thought I might be dreaming or going crazy. My most joyous realization was that I was fully awake and completely sane.

As I have reflected, the changes didn't all come at once. I think, like a computer coming back online, certain mental programs rebooted faster than others. Here is the sequence of how things rebooted in my brain.

My Brain Reboot Phase 1: Restarting My Perception

A few days after coming home from the hospital, I awoke in the morning, and everything seemed very big. The bedroom looked huge, and the ceiling looked higher. It was like I was seeing everything from a young child's point of view. As I looked around, I noticed things that previously I had overlooked. Colors and smells seemed more vivid, brighter, and impactful. It was like I was seeing and experiencing them for the very first time. Suddenly, I took nothing for granted.

I awoke one evening about 1 am and got out of bed. I looked up at the sky through the French doors in our bedroom. The night sky was full of stars, thousands of them. Each had a different brightness, slightly different color, and different depth. I stood there and marveled at the beauty. It was like I had never seen a night sky before. The truth was, I had, but I just never slowed down enough to really notice or appreciate it.

The next morning, I stood by my home office window looking out at the end of my neighbor's driveway. It was early, and the school bus had yet to arrive. While their mother stood quietly by, her three-year-old daughter and six-year-old son ran and played with the exuberance of youth. I heard the bus coming up the road, and the kids ran to greet it. Then, just before the little boy was about to board the bus, I watched his younger sister reach out and grab his hand. It was so sweet, just a simple gesture of love between sister and brother. My eyes welled up as I watched the beauty of that act. Before my brain reboot, I wouldn't even have noticed the kids at the end of the driveway.

There were so many things, big and small, that I experienced every day yet had never really taken the time to notice and appreciate. It was staggering how much I had missed, ignored, or just had been too busy and distracted to see.

My Brain Reboot Phase 2: Gaining Internal Perspective

As I was leaving the hospital, the doctors told me that I was at risk for developing blood clots from the inactivity of lying in a bed for five days. They told me the best thing I could do was to walk.

So, when I got home, I slowly shuffled around the house like a 90-year-old man. I paced from room to room trying to avoid dying from a stroke after just narrowly surviving COVID.

One morning, I shuffled my way through our dining room, and I saw a big bag of Sour Patch Kids candy sitting on the table. Prior to COVID, to me that bag of candy would have been like a vial of crack cocaine to a drug addict. I would have torn into it, and in minutes, half the bag would have been gone.

My broken brain would have been screaming to me, "Eat that candy; it will make you feel better. It will make you forget your brokenness and comfort you." Like a mindless zombie, I would have followed that advice until the sugar high overwhelmed me, and then I would have plopped down on the chair with a contented buzz.

Only this morning was different. I looked at that bag of candy and felt no urge to open it, no desire to feel that sugar high, no need to use it to hide from my brokenness. This behavioral shift was so striking that I had to ask myself, why? Why wasn't I ripping into that bag? Why did it suddenly have no power over me? What was driving that feeling?

Then it hit me. The reason I felt no desire for my candy vice was because I felt no brokenness. It was gone, erased. I still knew what happened to me in my childhood; however, I harbored none of the negative emotions associated with it.

All those years of carrying around fears, doubts, insecurities, anger, resentment, and a full, executive set of psychological baggage had suddenly come to a crashing halt. It was like a 1,000-pound weight had been lifted.

Interestingly, as this happened, for the first time in my life I could look at myself and my behaviors objectively. I could clearly see my vices and their root drivers. I could understand the full depth of my brokenness and the cause and effect of it. After 56 years of life, the blinders came off, and I could see the damage my brokenness had caused in my life and in the lives of those around me.

My Brain Reboot Phase 3: Fixing My Priorities

As my perspective shifted and I was able to see myself in a less negatively biased way, it caused me to truly understand the correlation between my limiting beliefs and my behaviors. At first, I used this perspective to examine my beliefs about myself; next, I began to examine my beliefs about success and what was truly important in my life.

I had spent the better part of my life subscribing to the notion that "more" was the end game of a life well lived. More money, more opportunity, more possessions, more recognition, more stuff. I fully bought into the idea that the key to happiness and fulfillment was going to be found in more of these external things. Strangely, it never occurred to me that, as I got more of any of these things, I never really felt any happier or more fulfilled. I never questioned it. I thought maybe I just needed a little "more" to get myself to that magical place of having and being enough.

Then one morning, I sat up in bed and looked out the window. It was like a tidal wave crashed over me. My whole life, everything that I had bought into, everything that I would have sworn was the absolute truth 30 days before, was a LIE.

More money, more worldly possessions, more recognition, and more stuff would never make me feel happier or more fulfilled. Having more of any of these things may make certain aspects of my life easier; however, in the grand scheme of life, they really didn't make a damn bit of difference. They weren't what success was; they weren't what was truly important in life.

Despite what the media, advertising, and manufacturing companies desperately want us to believe, there are only two things that truly matter in life, and neither can be bought or sold.

When the tidal wave crashed over me that morning, the next phase of my mental reboot happened. I realized that the two things that matter in life are *time* and *love*. These are the true measures of success. When we understand this, we have found the key to our personal happiness and fulfillment.

Understanding the True Value of Time   I once heard one of my coworkers, John Casey, say, "Time is the fairest thing in the universe. Highly successful and highly unsuccessful people get the same amount of it: 24 hours in a day, 1,440 minutes each day. Everybody gets the same amount."

We can't get more time, nor can we get it back once it has passed. It's gone, forever.

Before my reboot, I took time for granted, like it would always be there. I wasted it, spending countless hours on things that distracted me but in no way made me (or anyone around me) any better. I would sit mindlessly in front of the TV or in front of my computer screen, searching for something to entertain me, something that would make me laugh, something that would absorb my attention, and something that would distract me from my brokenness. Thousands on thousands of hours.

In this phase of the reboot of my brain, it dawned on me: I didn't want to waste any more time. I didn't want it to slip away without making a positive difference. With this insight, I began to reexamine how I was using each waking moment and what was important in that moment.

- Watching TV or mindlessly surfing the internet—not important
- Having a conversation with someone you love—very important
- Watching a YouTube video on the latest sports car or hottest new gadget—not important
- Watching a YouTube video that teaches you something insightful or expands your understanding—very important
- Getting swallowed up in the overwhelming negativity of the news or latest political crisis—not important
- Making a positive difference in the lives of the people around you—very important

After five decades walking the planet with mental blinders on, it finally dawned on me that happiness and success come when we use our time to make ourselves and those around us better.

Spreading Love You don't have to look hard to find negativity in the world. Fear, anger, disgust, and sadness run rampant on the 24-hour news channels, the media feeds on our phones, and the social media programs that we escape into. It is easy to become convinced that the world is one or more of the following:

- A place to be afraid
- Where we need to be ever-vigilant of that stranger to our right or left
- Wary of that person who has a different perspective
- Envious of people who have achieved more or live a different lifestyle than us
- Angry at people who are perceived as having wronged us or denied us opportunity
- Disgusted with people who don't share our opinions
- Saddened by the thought that we likely will never be able to escape our current situation

This was my world. It was what I saw. It was what I felt each day. This negativity consumed me and clouded my perspective from the second thing that truly matters: *love*.

As my brain rebooted, it occurred to me, I have no control over what is broadcast by the news channels, media feeds, and social media apps. If they want to portray our world as evil, uncaring, and negative, where we should be ever fearful, so be it. However, I get to choose what I let into my mind. I get to pick what I pay attention to. I get to decide if I want to see the world as one ruled by hate or love.

I also get to decide what I want to put back into the world: love or hate.

I once heard one of my peers, the business consultant Ken Blanchard, say, "Every decision we make and every action we take can bring either more love or more hate into the world." These words resonated in my mind as I finally realized that I get to choose if I want to make things better. I also realized that if I failed to make a conscious choice, in most cases, I would unconsciously make things worse.

If I wanted to be happier and more successful, I needed to consciously choose to bring more love into the world. I realized I needed to stop holding back and to tell the important people in my life about the greatness I saw in them. I needed to help the people I love to let go of fear and negativity. I needed to help them believe in themselves and what they can achieve.

The last thing the world needs is more fear and negativity. The last thing I needed was more fear and negativity. What we all need is more love and acceptance.

My Brain Reboot Phase 4: Living in the Present

I used to think I was a master at multitasking, juggling emails, projects, and requests all while in the midst of having a conversation with someone. Rarely, if ever, was I 100% focused on anything. Candidly, I would be surprised if I was 30% focused on anything. Yet I thought that was okay, necessary even, to get everything done, keep everybody happy, and, ideally, achieve what I wanted in life.

My mind was constantly bouncing from the negativity of my brokenness to what was immediately in from of me, to what needed to get done by the end of the week. The past, the present, and the future all swirled together in one jumbled mess in my head.

Through all of this, it never crossed my mind how this was perceived by those around me. I never thought about how it felt to my wife, kids, coworkers, and all the other people in my life to have the sense that they are only getting 30% of my attention? How does it feel to know the person you're speaking with is, at best, only moderately engaged in a conversation?

Consciously, I would never want someone to feel unimportant or unworthy of my full attention. Yet subconsciously, that was exactly what I was doing.

Through my brain reboot, my perspective, perception, and priorities all shifted in a positive direction. The last phase of the reboot centered me on the importance of being present, in the moment, and 100% engaged in what is most important at any given time.

I realized the concept of being good at multitasking is an illusion; it is a lie I told myself to make me feel important, productive, and successful. Ironically, it did the exact opposite of each of these things. This realization hit me hard as my brain rebooted.

Admittedly, at first, I wondered how I was going to be 100% present in conversations and still get anything done. Then I realized the reprioritization that had happened in phase 3 of the reboot had given me my time back. I simply wasn't wasting time on things that brought no meaning, benefit, or growth. I could spend more time really connecting in conversations, and I had the freedom to really focus, to be curious, and to ask deeper questions and truly listen.

For the first time in my life, I stopped focusing on what I wanted from the conversation and really worked to understand where someone else was coming from. My selfishness was replaced with compassion and empathy.

It was amazing how this changed the dynamics of my interactions with people. I saw them in an entirely new light, I saw what made them great, and I saw the brokenness that held them back. I saw their joy and felt their emotions. I experienced what it was like to really connect with them.

The Outcome of My Reboot

As I sit here this morning, it has been 23 days since they wheeled me out of the hospital. It is hard for me to comprehend the magnitude of how much my life has changed since this all began.

In my early 20s, I did a values assessment. It is a tool that helps you to clarify, define, and rank what was most important to you. *Peace of mind* topped my list. It was my highest value, what I desired most. Ironically, I never thought I would find it; I believed I would never escape my brokenness.

For the first time in 56 years, I know that peace of mind is not an illusion for me. The reboot of my brain has freed me of the pain and scars of my broken upbringing. I still know all that happened to me, yet I can look at it without all the negative emotion. I can't even find words to express how liberating that is.

These four phases of my mental reboot have shown me how to find the happiness and peace of mind that had eluded me my whole life.

As crazy as it may sound, I am incredibly grateful for having gone through the harrowing experience of struggling to breathe, being rushed to the hospital, and almost dying. Why? Because it taught me how to live.

CHAPTER 2

Doing Your Own Reboot

Have you ever found yourself second-guessing or doubting yourself? Have you ever really wanted to do something, achieve something, or pursue something, yet you just couldn't seem to get out of your own way and make it happen? How many times have you talked yourself out of doing something?

Likely, we've all found ourselves in that position of wanting to move our life in a given direction, yet we just can't seem to escape that little voice in our head telling us we aren't going to succeed. Maybe it pops up when we are trying to lose weight and get ourselves in shape. Perhaps, the doubts creep in when we are thinking of pursuing a new job or making a change in our career. Or perhaps that nagging little voice is keeping us from finding the relationship that we really want.

Everybody wants something, yet most seem to struggle to get it. Never really understanding how or why others seem to be able to move their lives in a better direction, but for some reason it just doesn't seem to work out for us.

If only there was an owner's manual for our mind, a set of instructions for ourselves. A simple guide that cuts through all the noise and, once and for all, enables us to understand the most important thing in our world—*us*. If only we could restart, reboot our thought process based on the right insights and right beliefs, it would make all the difference in the world. After all, if we can conquer our mind, we can conquer anything.

I don't think too many people would argue against the benefits of doing a brain reboot. After all, most of us hold some psychological baggage from our youth, upbringing, or even experiences in adulthood. It is this baggage that holds us back from not only being the person we want to be but also from living the life we want to lead.

With this being said, I am also enough of a realist to know that most people have no desire to risk death in order to be mentally reborn. Trust me, I don't blame them.

After my reboot was nearly complete, my new and improved mindset was settling in. I couldn't believe how much better everything seemed, and then a realization hit: I wanted nothing more than to find a way to help others experience what I was experiencing.

This is where my quest to write this book began. First, I reached out to the two most aware people I know: my mentor and his mentor. Next, I reached out to other experts I have met through my journey. I connected with doctors of psychology and neuroscience. I tapped into the leading minds in cognitive science. I was able to leverage the insights of Nobel Prize winners and the leading researchers of our day.

Through this journey, a picture began to emerge. I started to understand exactly what happened to me and why. I also was able to gain clarity regarding how others could replicate it within themselves (without the threat of death).

As I did the research, had the conversations, and wrote the words on these pages, I worked to simplify the complex, distill down the critical insights, and most important, explain why. Why are we the way that we are? Why do we struggle? Why do certain people succeed? Why are there a few simple adjustments in life that will always unshackle people? And the biggest why of all: why can we find happiness, peace of mind, and success through our own reboot?

So, are you ready? Are you ready to let go of the baggage? Are you ready to let go of the negative feelings and emotions? Are you ready to see what life really can look like when you are unencumbered by all that has held you back?

Are you ready to learn how to do your own brain reboot?

Okay, let's go . . .

PEOPLE–LEADER PERSPECTIVE

Not only is it possible to reboot oneself, but it is also possible to reboot an entire team. This is essentially equivalent to shifting a team culture in order to overcome a level of dysfunction, underperformance, or the need to move in a new direction.

Candidly, the single biggest source of resistance we battle as organizational leaders directly links back to issues that can be resolved only through mental rebooting. So if you are looking to move your team or organization in a new or better direction, read on. You will gain priceless insights into human performance and how to lead a team at the highest levels.

CHAPTER 3

The Brain You Were
Born With

M ost of us have some early memories of our childhood, such as having a birthday party or playing with friends. These memories may date back to when you were four or five years old. What we can't remember is how our brain worked when we were young. As such, we might assume that it worked just like it does now. However, nothing could be further from the truth.

When we are young, our brain works highly efficiently, unencumbered and uncluttered by negative thoughts or self-limiting beliefs. It processes information without skewing it, filtering it, or interpreting it based on any negative thoughts or limiting beliefs. When we are young, we see the world, ourselves, and everything that happens as it truly is, not based on any limitations. When we are young, the world we see is a profoundly different one, a better one.

Looking in the Mirror at the "You"
of Your Youth

We were not born to fail. We were born to learn. Both science and our own experience has proven this to be true.

At the time you came into the world, you were born with everything that you would need to build an incredible life for yourself. It was handed to you, gifted to you innately, and woven into your DNA.

Many people you will meet in your life will doubt these words. They will point to all those who struggle. They will cite example after example of people who have strived yet come up short, given up, and settled for mediocrity. Certainly, there is no shortage of people with dashed hopes, broken dreams, and shattered souls.

Yet none of us started out this way. Each of us came into life full of promise, energized by the opportunities and relentlessly willing to do whatever was necessary to fulfill our greatest desires.

Rest assured; you came into life with everything you need to succeed.

Consider this one simple yet indisputable fact: while you have learned thousands of things in your lifetime, two of the most difficult things you ever learned were prior to the age of two: walking and talking. Arguably these are the two most complex skills you will develop in your lifetime.

I want to take you back to when you were learning to walk.

One day, there you were crawling across the floor just looking around in wonderment at everything that you could see. Then you looked upward at the people around you, and a thought crossed your mind. "Hmm, they are walking, and here I am crawling across the floor. This crawling stuff is a little tough on the knees; maybe there is something to this walking thing."

So off you set on a new mission in life. You crawled over to the sofa, and with all your might you pulled yourself into a standing position. Propped up on your wobbly little legs, you looked around at this incredible new vantage point of the world. Then you glanced down at your hands grasping on to the edge of that sofa, and slowly you loosened your grip and moved your hands away.

Suddenly, the laws of physics took over. Gravity and a lack of balance reared and down you fell, hitting the floor with a loud thud. You sat there for a few seconds, stunned and dismayed. Slowly the stars started to clear from your head, and your vision refocused.

Did this sudden occurrence deter you? Did the shock of hitting the floor sway you from trying again?

Not in the least. So once again you propped yourself up, and once again, you fell.

Over and over, you went through this process, falling forward, backward, sideways, hundreds of times. With each fall, with each setback, and with each stumble you gained perspective, insights, knowledge, and eventually you learned. You learned about center of gravity and about balance, and slowly but surely, you put one foot in front of the other and you began to walk.

In a study published in the *Journal for Psychological Science*, researchers at New York University found that the average toddler will fall 17 times an hour as they are learning to walk. Over and over again, hour after hour, you fell hundreds, if not thousands, of times in order to perfect this intricate skill set.

Ask yourself, were these falls a symbol of your failure or were they a central part of your learning process?

The Swiss-American psychologist Elisabeth Kübler-Ross once said,

"There are no mistakes; all events are blessing given to us to learn from."

When you were a young child, nothing was viewed as a mistake, everything you did, every setback, every fall, taught you something important. Life was all about learning, adjusting, and adapting when you were a toddler; there was no judgment or beating yourself up when you fell down.

The amazing thing is, when you were a child, never once did you say to yourself, "Maybe these adults are supposed to walk, but I am meant to crawl." That negative thought never even crossed your mind.

Just look how you moved as a child. You were fearless, determined, goal-directed, motivated, inquisitive, and eager to learn. You didn't quit. You didn't give up. You didn't get a negative attitude. You didn't doubt yourself or your capabilities. You just relentlessly practiced until, eventually, you were able to walk.

Yes, it is painful to fall. Nobody enjoys stumbling. However, ask yourself, why did you willingly go through the pain and suffering of falling down over and over and over again?

You did it for one simple, yet incredibly important reason: you had unwavering belief in yourself. You didn't doubt yourself or have negative thoughts running through your head. You were confident in your abilities; you knew you could succeed. You were unstoppable.

When Everything Changed

REGAINING OUR RESOLUTION

Michelle and I had rented a beach house in Duck, North Carolina. It is a little community that sits on the barrier islands of the Outer Banks. Unfortunately, the weather wasn't cooperating, and we had more rainy and windy days than the sunny ones we were hoping for. So, we had decided to do some exploring of the area. What we discovered was that not far from where we were staying was the town of Kitty Hawk.

This may ring a bell in your mind because Kitty Hawk is the town where Orville and Wilbur Wright had flown the world's first airplane. The state of North Carolina had built a museum to commemorate the Wright brothers' achievement and its contribution to our society, so we decided to go and check it out.

It was a quiet day, so the director of the museum walked with us as we explored the exhibits and told us about the story of these two unlikely inventors and their journey that changed the world.

She told of how the brothers had become fascinated with the idea of flight in the 1870s when they saw a newspaper article about a German inventor who was trying to "fly like birds do."

Early in the process they decided that a fixed wing was going to work better than the more birdlike, movable wing approach that others had been trying for centuries before. They quickly realized they needed to find a wing design that provided lift characteristics. However, they also needed a scientific way to test wing designs. As such, their first invention wasn't an airplane, it was a wind tunnel.

Over and over, they tested different 12-inch-wide wing designs, trying to perfect the optimal profile. In total they tested more than 12,000 different designs until they discovered the perfect one.

Next, they had to find a way to build that wing design large and strong enough, yet lightweight enough, to lift a human being into the air. In total this process took them more than two decades of their lives, all so they could fly through the air for 12 seconds on the morning of December 17, 1903. From that point on the world was forever changed.

As we walked out of the back side of the museum, Michelle and I both marveled at the magnitude of the Wright brothers' achievement. It was so much more involved than either of us ever imagined.

Behind the museum, there is a large sand dune where they launched that first airplane that winter morning. On top of it now stands a monument commemorating their achievement.

As Michelle and I hiked up that sand dune toward the monument, I could see that there was an inscription carved into its base. It spoke to how the Wright brothers' dream was,

Achieved through dauntless resolution and unconquerable faith.

More than two decades later that inscription still stands indelible in my mind because dauntless resolution and unconquerable faith are the two ingredients required for every accomplishment of magnitude.

The reason each of us is able to walk, talk, read, and write is because we pursued those endeavors with dauntless resolution and unconquerable faith. Just imagine what we could make our lives look like if we pursued all of our dreams that way.

Our reboot will help us to once again find that ability.

Letting Go of the Fear of Failing

Why did you move the way you did as a child? Why were you willing to fall down over and over? Why did you keep standing back up instead of giving up?

Here's why. You see, as a small child you didn't know that it was possible to fail. The very concept of failure didn't even exist within your consciousness. We as adults did not yet have the chance to teach you about failure. Society had yet to place limits on your beliefs. In essence, you still possessed an unlimited mindset that is rooted in the belief that you could accomplish anything you set out to do. Although that may require falling down hundreds of times, you were willing to pay whatever dues were required to succeed.

You were born with everything you needed to succeed in life. You were born with a mindset that had no limits, no doubts, and no negativity. It was the mindset that allowed you to master one of the most complex skill sets you will ever learn in your lifetime. If you doubt that, let me just ask you this: How often do you crawl anymore?

Now, ask yourself this question: How many adults would be willing to fall down 17 times an hour if that was what was required to succeed at something? Very few. How many adults still possess the unwavering belief, the relentless determination, and the boundless self-motivation that once propelled their success as a two-year-old? Very few.

Most of the people you will meet in life will desperately want to cling to the chair like the toddler does when learning to walk—for them the chair offers the illusion of stability, while letting go requires them to face their fears of the unknown. They just don't want to let go. They don't want to get outside their comfort zones. They don't want to face the uncertainty of possibly making a mistake and falling down. Even if giving themselves permission to fall, in other words, to make a mistake, is the very key that will enable them to realize everything they most desire in life.

So, something must have changed in the way our brain works from the time we were children. Some shift must have occurred that causes us to doubt ourselves, to second-guess our capabilities, and to put boundaries on our ability to succeed.

What happened to us? Why did it happen? Most important, how can we change it back?

One of the most powerful things to realize is that we can choose how we think. In fact, we have to choose, if we want to succeed in life. Letting go of the excessive negativity, the fear of failing, and the incessant self-doubts that plague so many is your first and most important step to rebooting your brain and rediscovering who you "really" are. My reboot taught me this, and as we progress forward in our conversation, I'll share what goes wrong, why it goes wrong, and, most important, how you can do your own reboot and put everything right, once again.

PEOPLE–LEADER PERSPECTIVE

Fear is the most debilitating emotion when it comes to increasing organizational performance. As people leaders, we see the legacy of fear every time we are looking to make a change, shift a strategy, or introduce a new tool or application. Fear is the root cause of employee close-mindedness and the resistance to learning new skills and abilities.

Almost every single organizational challenge will ultimately distill down into a people-based problem (getting people to embrace change, use their time more effectively, collaborate better, be more engaged, resist less and adapt more, and so on). Helping employees to regain the mindset that they were born with is the only way to drive innovation and lead people to the highest levels. It is the underlying secret that every great people leader understands.

Imagine what your team could accomplish if, starting tomorrow, they did the following:

- Let go of their excuses
- Moved with a relentless persistence in solving problems and improving effectiveness
- Exhibited a quiet sense of unwavering confidence in their ability to learn and adapt
- Showed no fear of change
- Consistently moved with a boundless sense of self-motivation

These are the characteristics that are consistent with someone who has rebooted their perspective. These are the characteristics you will be able to foster by leveraging the insights you will learn moving forward in our conversation.

CHAPTER 4

What Goes Wrong with Our Brain and Why?

If the earliest version of our brain is perfect and if it is completely designed to help us build the life we most want for ourselves, what goes wrong? Why does it go awry? What happens?

As adults, why are we the way we are? Why do we think the way we do? Why do we feel the way we do? Why do we struggle? More important, why do we succeed? Why?

My quest to understand how to reboot the brain really started with this one fundamental question of why? Little did I know it would open a well of incredible insights.

Broadening Our Perspective on Ourselves

We humans tend to think of ourselves in a somewhat finite sense. One day we're born, and if good fortune smiles on us, 80 or 90 years later we pass away comfortably in our sleep. Throughout this journey, we will have moments of happiness and sorrow. We will laugh, and we will cry. We will face sicknesses and disappointments. We will experience joy, loss, and regret.

I always thought that over the course of that lifetime, we end up being who we are based on the sum total of all our life experiences. If we were blessed enough to have the right upbringing, a good education, the right contacts and relationships, good timing, and a little bit of luck on our side, then we would have a great life. Conversely, if we were born into a tough environment, if our parents didn't do such a great job, if the education system failed us, and lady luck looked the other away, then our life was pretty much destined to suck. I thought, that's just how it works, right?

Well, what if that wasn't the case? What if there were forces that shaped us, defined us, or, at the very least, profoundly affected who we would become long before we were even born?

No, I'm not talking about what the Hindus and Buddhists refer to as karma. I'm referring to something even more powerful: evolution.

As I was trying to understand the process of rebooting our brain, my research led me to Oxford University's evolutionary biologist Richard Dawkins. He shared a powerful insight relating to evolution when he said,

"Evolution only cares about one thing: survival of the species."

Within that one simple statement he opened a fundamental truth that led to a groundswell of insight into why we are the way that we are. Almost every aspect of who we are today is because it helped our ancestors to survive in their environment millions of years ago.

With the advent of modern medicine, we humans now have the potential to walk the planet for 80 or 90 years; however, we have all been shaped by the life experiences and environments that our ancestors have inhabited for close to 500 million years.

Evolution defined the way our body is shaped, the length of our arms and legs, our bone structure, and how our internal organs work. It defined the way our muscles work, how we walk, and how our hands grasp objects. In a physical sense, we are all a by-product of evolution; every aspect of us has an evolutionary purpose that helped our ancestors to survive, so it has been handed down from generation to generation for millions of years.

However, what the emerging field of evolutionary psychology is beginning to show us is that evolution didn't just shape our physical self; it also profoundly shaped our mental self. It was here that I began to find the answer to the question of why.

DISCOVERING OURSELVES

As I mentioned earlier, when I was 25 years old, I did a values assessment and ranked *peace of mind* as my number one value. Little did I know I picked one of the most elusive values possible. This is not because peace of mind is unattainable but rather because it is the last thing that humans were designed to find.

The simple truth is our minds, yours and mine, were never designed to provide us with peace of mind. It wasn't even something that was in the initial design specifications of our mind. In its purest sense, evolution designed our mind with just one goal: keeping us alive long enough so that we could create offspring and perpetuate the species. That's it.

Survival of the species, that's all evolution cares about. As evolution shaped every aspect of our ancestors, it didn't concern itself with our happiness, satisfaction, joy, a sense of accomplishment, or peace of mind. The only thing that mattered was keeping us safe and out of harm's way long enough for us to create more humans.

As Stanford University neuroscientist Andrew Huberman explained it to me, "we don't have to work for the negative; we are wired by evolution to find it. The circuits in our brain are more robust at calling it out. Subconsciously, we will automatically find it."

So, the focus of evolution and how it shaped our brain was to be ever-vigilant, on guard, wary of danger, and avoidant of anything that could potentially put us at risk. These were the things that kept our ancestors alive. Happiness, satisfaction, and joy were nice things to have but in no way necessary for the survival of the species.

That's not to say we can't find those more positive aspects of life; it is just important to understand our brain was never designed to help us in that regard. To find happiness, satisfaction, joy, a sense of accomplishment, or even peace of mind, we have to work around the way our brain was designed.

Understanding the Aspects of "You" That Evolution Cares About

If the launching point to our reboot begins with the influence of evolution, the next question was, how did evolution shape our brain and why?

This question led me to the research of Dr. Paul MacLean. MacLean was a neuroscientist who taught at Yale Medical School and ran the Laboratory of Brain Evolution for the United States National Institute for Mental Health. He seemed like a pretty good source.

MacLean proposed an easy-to-understand evolutionary model for how our brain evolved. He called it the *triune brain*. Basically, it is a simplified three-phase process that brought us to the three-pound brain that floats in our head today. Each of the three evolutionary phases served a specific purpose that was critical for our ancestors' survival in that given time period. As MacLean described it, first we evolved our survivor brain, next came our communicator brain, and then finally, the solver/ critical brain.

Your Survivor Brain

Everything we come to know about the world—every sight, every sound, everything we touch, taste, or smell—flows into the brain through our brain stem. It is the on-ramp from which sensory inputs move from our outside world into our internal world.

Our brain stem and the parts of the brain that immediately connect to it make up our *survivor brain*. MacLean and many other neuroscientists believe this to be the oldest part of the brain. It was the first portion of the brain that evolution began to develop.

The sapling that became our family tree began to grow about 5 million years ago. It was our ancestors' survivor brain that to no small extent is the reason we are alive and able to read these words today.

What does our survivor brain do for us? Stanford University neuroscientist Karl Pribram jokingly explained that it is primarily concerned with the four *F*s that are required for survival of the species:

- Fight
- Flight
- Food
- F&@king

I'll let you guess the fourth *F* (hint: it rhymes with *ducking*).

These are the four most important aspects of survival of the species. They were what was required 5 million years ago to ensure the gene pool continued to the next generation. Thus, they represent what evolution cared most about.

The bestselling author Ernessa T. Carter once said,

"No matter how evolved humans think they are, we still have the same fight-or-flight instincts of our caveman ancestors."

The Oldest and Most Intelligent Part of You

Although our specific family tree began to grow about 5 million years ago, our survivor brain actually began its evolutionary process long before our genus emerged. Today, many experts believe that the roots of our survivor brain trace back more than 500 million years. That easily makes it the oldest and most evolved part of our body.

TIME EMPOWERS EVOLUTION

Think about your first cell phone. Mine was a Motorola DynaTAC that I bought in the early 1990s.

Source: George / Adobe Stock.

(continued)

Coming in at right around two pounds, it was nicknamed the *brick phone* because of its size, shape, and weight. For its day, it was a marvel of technology: it didn't have to be hardwired in your house, you could carry it with you, it had a battery so it didn't need to be constantly plugged in, and you could make calls on the emerging early cell phone network for about $1 per minute, if you could find a signal (no easy guarantee on that).

However, that brick phone was a dinosaur compared to my modern iPhone. All the DynaTAC could do was make phone calls (and it didn't even do that particularly well). There was no internet access, text messaging, GPS directions, music, camera, or any of the other incredible features of our modern phones. In comparison to today's smartphones, my DynaTAC was truly pretty dumb.

Source: Kaspars Grinvalds / Adobe Stock.

In three short decades, our phones have gotten 82% lighter and smaller, they've also evolved into virtual supercomputers that enable us to instantaneously get an answer to any question, get directions wherever we want to go, and get in contact with people from around the world. With each new yearly evolution, our modern smartphones get more advanced, lighter, and increasingly powerful.

This is what 30 short years of evolution has done for the advancement of cell phone technology. Now, imagine what 500 million years of evolution has done to the power of your survivor brain.

The Intelligence of Our Survivor Brain

From the earliest days of modern psychology, it was believed that what motivated our flight-or-fight mechanism was external environmental factors. In other words, if our ancestors were walking along through the jungle and they came on a roaring lion, it would trigger a strong desire to run for their lives (flight). Yet, if they came on a sleeping lion, they might see it as on opportunity to eat, so they would fight to slay the slumbering beast.

However, in the late 1950s, Harvard researcher Dr. David McClelland began to question the commonly held believe that it was purely external environmental factors that drove our fight or flight motivation. McClelland posed the question, "If external factors motivate human behaviors, how can two people face the exact same external challenges and yet respond in opposite ways? One might give up at the slightest sign of resistance, while the other would dig in their heels and doggedly persist in overcoming the obstacle." He theorized that our ability to manage our thoughts and beliefs must be the cause of human motivation. The challenge was, in the 1950s, our limited understanding of the exact mechanisms by which the brain worked made McClelland's insight impossible to prove at that time.

It would take another 60 years before we possessed the ability to study the exact workings of the brain. In 2016, neurologist Aaron Boes and a team of researchers at Harvard were doing functional magnetic resonance imaging brain scans, and they discovered the process by which McClelland's supposition actually worked. With this finding, they uncovered our first and most evolved form of human intelligence. Our survivor brain works based on our *motivational intelligence* (MQ).

Our MQ is our awareness of and ability to manage negative thinking and self-limiting beliefs.

MQ forms the filter with which you and I perceive the world. Every input we receive through our five senses flows into our survivor brain first. This portion of the brain looks at that input and determines if it should be perceived as a threat or an opportunity. If at all possible, our survivor brain causes us to avoid perceived threats (flight) and to move toward opportunities (fight). At the end of the day, every action that we take is driven by our motivational intelligence.

The bottom line is, **our dominant thoughts and beliefs always drive our actions**. Remember this point—it is a critical one that we will circle back to later—it is a secret key to rebooting your brain.

PEOPLE–LEADER PERSPECTIVE

For you and me, as people leaders, there is nothing more important to understand than the emerging field of motivational intelligence. Why? For the simple reason that there is nothing that more directly correlates with employee performance than MQ. We see the influence of MQ every day across our team, we value it in our strongest performers, we are frustrated by the lack of it in the people who struggle, yet we have only come to understand its impact and how to positively influence MQ over the last handful of years.

As we journey forward in our discussion, we will create a deeper understanding of MQ and explore the proven ways that we, as leaders, can influence it. This insight will play a key role in recruiting effectiveness, employee retention, and engagement, fostering organizational agility and driving innovation and performance.

Your Communicator Brain

"Alone we can do so little. Together we can do so much."
—Helen Keller

From our survivor brain, MacLean theorized the second phase of brain development was our communicator brain. It is believed that this part of our brain began to evolve about 250 million years ago. Our communicator brain sits immediately on top of our survivor brain and is located right in the center of your skull. If you make a fist right now (go ahead, I'll wait), your fist is just about the same size and shape as your communicator brain.

So why do we have a communicator brain? Well, in a danger-laden time frame, where predators abound and threats lurks around every bend, survival is far from ensured. Evolution understood that as singular individuals roaming the plains of Africa our chances were pretty bleak. However, if we came together in packs, as small groups, we could protect one another. We could help one another to find food and avoid dangers.

However, for a group to help one another, it needs to be able to communicate. Yet, millions of years ago, our ancestors hadn't evolved enough to conceive of the notion of language. Evolution helped us to solve this critical challenge by creating the very first form of communication. It wasn't through words; no, the very first way we learned to communicate with one another is through emotions. We learned to read emotions on one another's faces; this was how we communicated danger or safety to one another hundreds of millions of years ago.

The First Form of Communication

In 1872, English biologist, Charles Darwin first theorized that emotions were universal to all human beings. A century later, University of California psychologist Paul Ekman was able to prove that we read emotions on one another's faces. The interesting thing was, for survival, we didn't need to have hundreds of different emotions. In fact, Ekman showed that evolution gave us just six root universal emotions. To this day, we share these base-level emotions with every other human being on the planet:

- Fear
- Anger
- Sadness
- Disgust
- Surprise
- Happiness

These are the six emotions we read on one another's faces. These are the emotions evolution created to foster our ancestor's survival.

Look back at these emotions. Are you noticing anything? Think about it for a second. What is it?

Right, four of our six universal emotions are decidedly negative (fear, anger, sadness, and disgust). Surprise could be either good or bad. The only universally positive emotion that evolution gave us was happiness.

Isn't that curious? Why would evolution have given us more negative emotions than positive ones?

Remember, what does evolution care about?

Right, the survival of the species, that's it.

If you go back millions of years ago, negative things were much more likely to kill our ancestors. As University of Chicago psychology professor Mihaly Csikszentmihalyi explains it, "Our ancestors learned to assume the worst because the worst tended to happen. Avoiding the worst kept them alive."

So, we developed more negative emotions as a necessary way to express threats, dangers, and bad things through our facial muscles. This was how we protected one another and how we perpetuated survival of the species.

Look at emotions like a volume control in the mind. They can turn up or down our level of urgency or sensory alertness with the release of chemicals in the brain. These chemicals (endorphins, dopamine, serotonin, and oxytocin) are evolution's pharmacy. Endorphins and dopamine act as stimulants to heighten our ability to fight or flight, and serotonin and oxytocin relax us and make us feel safe.

The Intelligence of Our Communicator Brain

In the early 1960s, while conducting research at Cornell University, Professor Michael Beldoch began noticing that certain people seemed to be better equipped to manage their emotions. This ability to observe, detect, and mindfully override emotions seemed to have positive impact on both a person's psychological stability and their effectiveness in communicating with other people.

Beldoch referred to his discovery as *emotional intelligence* (EQ). Our EQ is the intelligence of our communicator brain.

EQ is the second filter of the mind. External inputs hit our survivor brain first, and our dominant thoughts and beliefs determine if the sensory input represents a threat or opportunity to us.

This perception next flows into the communicator brain, and an emotion gets assigned to it.

People with higher EQ are subject to the same emotions as all of us. Remember, we all have the same six universal emotions. These emotions combine to create hundreds of feelings (joy, sorrow, regret, longing, contentment, guilt, security, sorrow, and so on), and we all experience these at varying times in our life. People with higher EQ are more aware of these feelings and the underlying emotions that drive them. They are also better able to intercept and redirect negative emotions and feelings before they morph into behaviors that could negatively affect the life they are working to build.

Conversely, people with lower EQ wear their emotions and feelings very close to the surface. They will tend to be more reactionary when it comes to negative emotions and feelings. This can cause more dramatic mood swings and destructive behaviors.

BREAKING AWAY FROM THE BAGGAGE

Through my brain reboot, I realized how my upbringing and the challenges it wrought had caused me to develop a lot of negative thinking and limiting beliefs. As such, much of the time I felt threatened, defensive, and on guard, leading to a groundswell of negative emotions.

You couldn't see the scars from the outside, yet inside they were very real to me. This caused me to have too much of a hair-trigger response that frequently came out as anger and resulted in me yelling, saying things I would later regret, and inflicting damage on those I loved.

Oddly, I was largely oblivious to the ripple effect of my behaviors. I was too caught up in my own issues, insecurities, and psychological baggage. Sure, once I calmed down, got my shit together, and could think in a more rational manner, I could see the damage I inflicted. However, when I felt threatened, my negative emotions got triggered, and I struggled to get them under control.

What I realized through my reboot was that rejection was a major trigger, or perceived threat, for me. I believe this is true for many people who experience trauma similar to mine. We desperately want to feel accepted, loved, and "good enough." It was as though our lack of being "good enough" brought on all of the trauma we endured as children. I thought I was the cause of my trauma, and if I was just a little bit better, then it wouldn't have

(continued)

happened; my childhood would have turned out better, and this would have positively flowed into who I became as an adult.

In reality, what happened to me, what happens to many of us (perhaps most of us in some form or another) as children isn't our fault. We are not responsible for it. We do not cause it. We have it inflicted on us by other broken people who are themselves dealing with their baggage. Sadly, though, this doesn't stop their psychological baggage from becoming our baggage.

Not until my reboot did I realize that I was carrying generations' worth of psychological baggage handed down from one person to the next. One of the greatest outcomes of rebooting my brain was the realization that I had the power (and the responsibility) to once and for all put that baggage away and break the cycle.

PEOPLE–LEADER PERSPECTIVE

EQ plays a significant role in relationship building and communication effectiveness. Leaders who exhibit higher levels of EQ have empathy, tend to be better listeners, and thus can connect on a deeper level with their teams.

Your Solver/Critical Brain

In MacLean's model of the brain's evolution, the final phase was our solver/critical brain. From a human perspective, this portion of our brain is estimated to be just 4 to 5 million years old.

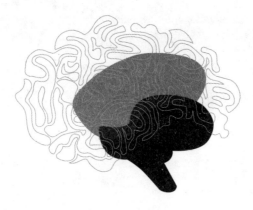

Once our brain had evolved a way to focus on the four *F*s of survival (fight, flight, food, and f&@king) and a means of communicating with the rest of our pack (emotions), it began to focus on higher-level challenges like developing tools to make life easier, creating shelter from the harsh elements, mastering fire, and ultimately, developing a spoken language.

All of these tasks fell to the third aspect of our brain, the solver/critical brain. It is a half-inch-thick membrane that wraps around our communicator and survivor brain. If you have ever seen an image of the outside of a human brain, you can't help but notice it looks a lot like hamburger. What you're looking at is the solver/critical portion of the brain.

The Troublemaker of the Mind

Our solver/critical brain is where logic, strategy, planning, and goal direction lives. It is in this part of our brain where we are able to visualize the future and think about the things that we can do today to influence it. It is also the part of the brain that holds our positive and negative thoughts, those very thoughts that all too often cause us to second-guess ourselves and question the decisions we make.

Compared to the rest of our mind, our solver/critical brain is a relative infant from an evolutionary standpoint. Like a toddler trying to navigate their way through the terrible twos, our solver/critical brain often wreaks havoc on our perception and satisfaction with our life. As we journey forward in our conversation, much of discussion will center on how we can wrest control from this cranky, second-guessing aspect of our mind.

The Intelligence of Our Solver/Critical Brain

In 1905, French psychologist Alfred Binet became one of the first researchers to quantify the intelligence of our solver/critical brain. He created a test to measure reasoning and logic skills, which became the first accepted means of evaluating human intelligence.

Our cognitive and reasoning abilities are the intelligence of our solver/critical brain. Today, we have come to know this as a person's intelligence quotient (IQ). We often refer to these on a numeric scoring system that ranges between about 50 and 200+. The average, in most industrialized countries, will fall between 85 and 115. For reference, someone is classified as a genius if their IQ exceeds 160 (it is reputed that Albert Einstein had an IQ of 164).

This form of intelligence is where that little voice in your head lives. Yes, you can admit it (I'll keep it our little secret)—we all talk to ourselves all day long. That little voice is rambling on most of our waking hours, critiquing, judging, and commenting on virtually everything that we are experiencing through our five senses at any given time. Most people don't realize how much the narrator in their head influences every aspect of their life—and not necessarily in a positive way.

THE CRITICAL LITTLE VOICE

"You can't do that . . ." "They shouldn't treat you that way . . ." "Can you believe what they just did?" "How could they . . . ?" "This isn't going to work out . . ." "You don't want to . . ." "Oh no, not now . . ." "Wouldn't you rather . . . ?" "You're not . . ."

So often that little voice in my head was guiding me to stay safe, avoid risks, take the easy pathway, look for the shortcut, do what was most immediately pleasurable. On the surface these things might not seem like such a bad idea. After all, what could be wrong with playing it safe, looking for an easy way out, or just outright avoiding making a mistake?

My mentor once said to me, "What looks like the easy path up-front always becomes the hard path in the end. What looks like the hard path up front always turn out to be the easier path in the end."

My little voice was always leading to what ultimately turned out to be the hardest path. This is what our brain does; in many ways it is a default process of the mind. A process that kept our ancestors alive but today, in a vastly different world than the one our ancestors inhabited, it frequently confines us to a life of unease, uncertainty, and, ultimately, mediocrity. But it doesn't have to. What I discovered in my reboot is that you and I can overcome the hardwiring of the past and shape our lives in profoundly better ways.

PEOPLE–LEADER PERSPECTIVE

From a leadership perspective, there are two important insights regarding the solver/critical brain, and the intelligence that drives it, that we need to understand.

First, IQ plays a much smaller role in a person's success than most realize. As we discussed, in the industrialized world, the average IQ range will be between 85 and 115. What researchers have shown is that if a person has an IQ between 105 and 115 (just the upper end of average), they can do any job, including being a rocket scientist or a brain surgeon. So you don't need to have a genius-level IQ to be successful in any given role. Ultimately, motivational intelligence has the biggest impact on success, followed by emotional intelligence; IQ is a distant third.

Second, individuals who have backgrounds in more technically oriented or logic-based roles (engineering, software development, legal, and so on) will tend to lean into more of their IQ/solver/critical brain. Oftentimes this will help them to excel when they are in more frontline roles; however, in many cases it will hurt them when they move into people leadership roles. This is not to say they can't become great people leaders, just that they must work harder to leverage their emotional intelligence and understand how to develop the motivational intelligence of their people.

What Evolution Handed You and Me

As shocking as it may seem, we are much less a product of our environment or a product of our parent's genetics than we may think. In reality, virtually every aspect of us, both physically and mentally, is a by-product of the environment our ancestors lived in millions of years ago.

Yet, the world our ancestors lived in was vastly different than the modern one we live in. The things that threatened them no longer threaten us today. Although people still go hungry, modern-day agriculture has enabled us to feed a large portion of the planet. With rare exception, humans are not killed by predatory animals who stalk us for food. Most of us have shelter from the extreme elements of nature.

All of this has happened in just the last 12,000 years. Although that may seem like a very, very long time, it represents only about 3% of the life span of our species as homo sapiens, .2% of the 5 million years that our family tree has been growing, and .000024% of the time evolution has been shaping our brain.

What does all this really mean for us today? In simple terms, evolution hasn't designed the intelligence that drives our brain for the world we live in today. It hasn't taken into account the pace of our world, the rate of change, the quantity of data we have to process, the influence of social media, or any other factor we deal with in our modern society.

CHAPTER 5

Modern Life with Our Ancient Mind

As a species, every day we learn more, discover more, and create more. This process has dramatically accelerated since the dawning of the digital age just five short decades ago. Today, you, me, and the rest of our peers generate a mind-boggling amount of new information and new data every single day—1.15 trillion megabytes of data each day in fact (which I discovered in a 45-second Google search on data).

Collectively, we create more data and more information in 24 hours than every one of our ancestors did across millions of years of existence. All of this data accumulates on servers around the world and informs our news feeds, social media, and internet searches. We consume it through our televisions, laptops, tablets, smartphones, and every other connected device we own. You and I are immersed in an endless sea of information.

All of this information feeds the 60,000 odd thoughts that flow through our mind each day and serves to influence how we come to perceive the world, other people, and ourselves. However, what I came to understand through my reboot is these thoughts aren't merely transient realizations, perspectives, judgments, or critiques. They are much more powerful than I previously realized.

In the mid-1800s, the American essayist, lecturer, and poet Ralph Waldo Emerson wrote:

Watch your thoughts, they become your words.
Watch your words, they become your actions.

Watch your actions, they become your habits.
What your habits, they become your character.
Watch your character, it becomes your destiny.

But how and why do our passing thoughts become our destiny?

Our thoughts, when held over time, reflected on, and repeated over and over, begin to shape our beliefs. Our beliefs become our central referencing point for everything. They define what we see as our truth. Our truth determines what we perceive as threats or opportunities.

Previously we talked about how evolution has left us with a mind that is programmed for survival a million years ago. It's a mind that is ever-vigilant, on guard, critical of taking risks, wary of perceived threats, and abhors uncertainty.

We now live in world that is changing faster than in any other time in history. It's a time wrought with uncertainties where the best path forward will nearly always involve taking risks.

Think about it: How will we ever build a meaningful relationship if we are fearful of taking the risk of talking to that person on the other side of the room? How will we ever build a successful career if we are unwilling to take the risk of going after that promotion, looking for a better job, or pursing our entrepreneurial dream? Almost everything meaningful starts with uncertainty, risk, and the threat of falling on our face.

The funny thing is, as children, the prospect of falling on our face didn't faze us at all. Yet as adults, it scares the crap out of us. What changes in us from the time we are a fearless toddler to cautionary adult?

It was with this question in mind that a friend from Omaha introduced me to Nobel Prize–winning psychologist Daniel Kahneman. Kahneman has spent decades of his career studying hedonic psychology. That sounds impressive and maybe a little confusing, right? Here's what it really is all about. It's the study of what makes us perceive our life as pleasant or unpleasant. It is what causes us to experience sorrow or joy, satisfaction or dissatisfaction. Basically, it is what causes us to experience the world the way we experience it.

What I was looking for from Daniel was to help me understand how our ancient mind works in this modern world. Man, did he ever deliver.

What he helped me understand was the incredible influence our thoughts and beliefs have on how our brain works. Here is how it all comes together. **Catch this: it's really important for your reboot.**

Our upbringing, societal influences, and life experiences create the dominant thought patterns that, over time, form the set of beliefs we hold on just about everything. We have beliefs about who we are and how the world works. We have beliefs about our capabilities and weaknesses. We have beliefs about other people, money, health, relationships, government, and so forth. Our whole perception of *everything* is based on our beliefs.

Here is the wild thing. Are you ready to have your mind blown?

Your beliefs are the basis of everything your life has become, everything you know, everything you perceive, and everything that you expect and assume is going to happen to you. Yet, these beliefs—your beliefs— are entirely unique to you; although some other people may share certain beliefs with you, nobody on the planet shares every one of your exact beliefs.

Your beliefs are your reality . . . and in all likelihood . . . they aren't all true. And this is where our brain goes astray.

THE TIES THAT BIND

It was the last full day of our vacation in Naples, Florida, and Michelle and I were searching for some memorable way to wrap up our trip. We stood in our hotel lobby going through the brochure rack, looking at all the local attractions and trying to make a decision.

Michelle pulled out a brochure for Jungle Larry's Zoological Park. As she looked it over, she noted that they claimed to have the "world's best petting zoo." Well, that pretty much sealed the deal; we were going to Jungle Larry's.

When we got there, it was set up in a big semicircle. We paid our admission fee and set off. We saw the lions and the tigers, the bears, and the monkeys. Then we came around a bend, and there was the petting zoo.

I walked in and did a quick scan of the animals. They had all the typical ones you see in a petting zoo. There were goats, a couple of donkeys, some rabbits, and sheep. However, in the very back of the petting zoo was an animal I had never had a chance to pet before. It was an elephant.

(*continued*)

I'm not sure if you've ever been up close to an elephant before; if you haven't, there are a couple of things that strike you when you get close to them. First, TV doesn't do justice to how big these animals are; they are absolutely immense creatures. The second thing that strikes you is when you reach out to pet them, they don't feel like you think they are going to feel. They have all these prickly, coarse hairs on them.

As I am petting this elephant's ear, I notice that there is an elephant handler leaning up against a fence by the elephant's head. So, I decided to strike up a conversation with her.

I asked her, "How big is this elephant?" She explained that this was an African elephant, and they can get up to about 12 or 13 feet tall. Next, I asked her, "How much do they weigh?" She said they can weigh upwards of 14,000 pounds.

I just stood there astonished, and then I looked down and something struck me as very curious. I noticed that the elephant had a rope tied around its right front ankle. The roped snaked across the ground and other end of it was tied around a wooden stake that had been pounded into dirt. The rope was about the thickness of my pinky finger.

I took a closer look, and I noticed that the rope looked like the only thing that was holding that elephant in place. Now, it didn't take a genius-level IQ to figure out that if that elephant wanted to go someplace, that stinking little rope wasn't going to slow it down one bit.

When, I made this observation to the elephant handler, she gave a me knowing smile. Obviously, I wasn't the first "Einstein" to point this out to her.

Then she explained something to me that I have never forgotten.

She said that when the elephants are just babies, they keep them in a large pen with a metal shackle around their right front ankle. That shackle has a chain attached to it that is anchored in cement in the very center of the pen.

She explained that the baby elephants will walk as far as they can until they get to the end of the length of chain. Then they will pull on the chain and realize that they can't walk any farther. She said this will go on for a couple of weeks; however, after that the baby elephants realize that they can't walk any farther, so they stop pulling on the chain.

She told me that elephants have a tremendous memory. It's so good in fact that they will remember this lesson for the balance of their lifetime. They remember it so well that anytime they are tied up with anything around their right front leg, as long as they can see it, they won't try to get away, because they have become conditioned to believe that they can't.

I thought that was a pretty amazing story.

Well, the next day, Michelle and I were on a plane heading back home. I began to reflect on what that elephant trainer had told me the day before. As I was thinking about this, something hit me like a ton of bricks.

What I realized is that in so many ways, I had been conditioned just like that elephant. Somewhere along the way in my life I was told by a guidance counselor that I wasn't smart enough to take this class or that class. I was told by a coach that I wasn't good enough to place first string. I was told by a girl that I wasn't cute. I was told that I shouldn't set my standards too high. I was told that I didn't have musical aptitude. I was told a lot of things, and for whatever reason, I inadvertently chose to believe these things.

All of these beliefs conspired together to shape the way I perceived myself and my capabilities. This in turn informed my choices and the decisions I made. My beliefs shaped my world.

I never thought to question them; they were my beliefs, they had to be correct, and they must be true or else why would I believe them?

In fact, I believed them so much, that I could think of countless times I wouldn't even try something, simply because I didn't believe I could do it. Bam, I was conditioned just like that elephant.

I thought about Michelle, and I realized she had been conditioned the same way. I thought about my friends and realized they had been conditioned same way. Then I realized that pretty much all of us have been told who we are, what we are, what we're capable of (and not capable of), and with that our beliefs about ourselves become conditioned.

Our beliefs become our truth—just not necessarily the real truth.

About two months after my mental reboot, I was still trying to process what had happened to me and why. I had spoken to countless people about my experience; they all seemed somewhat in awe as I explained my revelations, yet they all were at a loss as to why this had occurred.

Then one afternoon, I was speaking with Dr. Emma Davies, a friend and colleague in Australia. As I was detailing my story, she very matter-of-factly said, "You're experiencing post-traumatic growth, or PTG."

Somewhat confused, I said, "I've heard of post-traumatic stress disorder (PTSD), but what is post-traumatic growth?"

She helped me to understand that recent research had discovered that human beings have a range of responses to traumatic experiences. On the far negative side is PTSD; on the more positive side is PTG. She had actually extensively researched PTG as a post-grad while earning her PhD in psychology, and thus was somewhat of an expert.

Next, she explained that what had happened as a result of the trauma of struggling to breathe, being hospitalized, and coming close to death was my motivational intelligence had rebooted itself. This reset my perceptions, negative thought patterns, and the limiting beliefs that I had inadvertently built my life around. In essence, it wiped the slate clean and gave me a fresh start. Five decades after I was born, I had the advantage of being reborn as an adult with a renewed perspective and without the baggage of my past.

It was this conversation with Emma that showed me the pathway to help others to reboot themselves (without the trauma). It showed me what you and I need to focus on to facilitate your reboot. So, if you're ready, read on.

PEOPLE–LEADER PERSPECTIVE

On both a micro level (individual performance) and macro level (team/ organizational performance), MQ is the governor of success. How effectively people and teams manage negative thinking and limiting beliefs will define every aspect of how they act and react every day.

Over the years, much has been written about the importance of developing an optimal culture. Yet leaders around the globe still struggle to understand and guide culture. Why? Partially because they lack a good working definition of what a culture is and rarely are they taught the tools whereby they can positively affect their team culture.

A culture is the collective set of dominant thoughts and beliefs. Considering this definition, it is easy to see that each of us as individuals have a culture of dominant thoughts and beliefs that live in our mind. When a group of people come together in a team, over time, they will also lock onto a shared set of dominant thoughts and beliefs, and this becomes the culture of the team.

In our conversation ahead, we will discuss the exact beliefs we need to influence to unshackle our people's performance and to foster an optimal team culture.

PART 2

Becoming the New You: Your Mental Reboot

Maximizing the Impact of Your Reboot

More than 3,000 hours of in-depth research in the fields of neuroscience and cognitive psychology have gone into the next part of our conversation. Every portion of our discussion exists for a specific purpose and is designed to help you in your rebooting journey. Rest assured, nothing has been left to chance.

There are three critical elements woven throughout our conversation. I want to point them out up-front to make sure you leverage them to their full effect.

- **Questions.** There are a number of questions in each section of our discussion. Please don't just read through them just to get to the next sentence. Every time you come upon a question, I want to encourage you to really stop and think about it. Consider your perspective and your thoughts relating to the question. These questions are there to really make you think. Your thoughts and the realizations they will yield are designed to help you rewire important aspects of your awareness.

- **Quotes.** Throughout our conversation I have leveraged the insights of many of the most accomplished people throughout history. Let their words, insights, and wisdom guide you. Take the time and reflect on these quotes. Each has been chosen for a very specific purpose. They are not idle words on a page; these quotes are the most sage advice from history's most accomplished people. Let these luminaries be your mentors. Let their words guide your thoughts.
- **Stories.** After each important point, I have used stories to help you tie down and remember some critical insight. The stories are there to show the cause and effect of key concepts and to demonstrate how these points ripple in our daily life. Our brain is designed to remember stories, so this part of our conversation is a critical aspect designed to stay in your long-term memory.

CHAPTER 6

For Your Reboot: The Power of Choice Is Your Most Important Asset

There are two things that separate us, as humans, from virtually everything else on the planet. The first is opposable thumbs (a trait we share with a handful of primates, koala bears, and some South American tree frogs). However, it's the second trait that truly makes us uniquely human. It is our ability to process information and make conscious choices based on it.

Our power of choice is our greatest asset in life. It's our ability to choose that enables us to reboot our thought process and forever improve our life. It gives us the ability to steer, move, and guide our life in any given direction. Regardless of circumstances, situations, hardships, history, or obstacles, we have the ability, the power, and, most important, the responsibility to choose the way we interpret them and how we respond.

Certainly, some people will have advantages that we don't have. Others will face obstacles that we don't. Our ability to choose is the greatest equalizer in life. The choices we make enable us to level the playing field and find ways to succeed regardless of circumstance.

More than 200 years ago, the great statesman Thomas Jefferson said,

"We are all born with the equal ability to be unequal."

Regardless of where we find ourselves today, we can be someplace different, someplace better tomorrow. However, the only way we will get there is by changing ourselves first. This is why our rebooting process is essential for shifting the direction of our life. The way we choose to think, the things we choose to believe, what we decide to focus on, what we feed into our mind always translates into the actions that we take in life.

However, don't take my word for all of this. Just look back in history; every major shift in humankind can be attributed to people who thought and acted differently. These are the people who are noted and spoken about. Interestingly, the people who chose to think like everyone else are never written about. Why? Simply, because they made little difference. They made little difference in their own lives and in the lives of those around them.

The Power of What We Choose to Believe

The real question is, why? Why do some people act and react in a different way, a better way, a way that enables them to get better outcomes than other people? That is a complex question with a very simple answer.

People act the way they do based solely on what they have come to believe—what they have come to believe about themselves, about those around them, and about the way they believe the world works. Understand that these thoughts and beliefs, the ones that we hold so dear, may be entirely flawed. They may be absolutely inaccurate, but nevertheless, they still govern every aspect of how we move through the world.

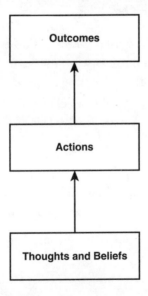

More than 2,500 years ago, Gautama Buddha established a philosophy that became the foundation of the Buddhist religion. One of the central tenets of Buddhist teachings is based on the concept of causality or karma. The Buddha understood that our inner world drove the actions we took in our outer world. The sum of our actions determines our future.

Two hundred years later and halfway around the world from where Buddha lived, the great Greek philosopher Aristotle also spoke at length about how our beliefs were the central cause of the outcomes of our lives.

In 1687, the English physicist and mathematician Sir Isaac Newton published his third law of physics, which is talked about in every school around the world and is the basis for the familiar saying "For every action there is an equal and opposite reaction." This is perhaps better known as the law of cause and effect.

The central theme that has rung true for more than 2,500 years is that things don't just happen, they happen for a reason.

People don't succeed and people don't fail by accident. They succeed or fail for a reason. People don't win or lose by accident. They win or lose for a reason. People don't strive for greatness or struggle in mediocrity by accident. They strive or struggle for a reason. People aren't happy or unhappy by accident; they are happy or unhappy for a reason. People don't find peace of mind by accident; they find peace of mind for a reason. That reason is always rooted in their thoughts and beliefs.

IN THE AGGREGATE, MENTAL MOMENTUM MATTERS MOST

There I was sitting in the parking lot at the Eastview Mall waiting for my business partner and mentor, Joe Gianni, to show up. We had a long drive to get to a client meeting and I didn't want to be late.

He came wheeling into the parking lot and I got into the passenger seat of his car. He looked at me and with great enthusiasm said, "You know, I've been thinking a lot about something."

"What's that?" I asked.

He said, "Everything in life is cumulative. We tend to look at things as singular events, but then they all add together and begin to make a big difference."

I don't know that I fully grasped that concept that day in the mall parking lot. However, as I have reflected over time, I have come to realize how profound his words were that day.

(continued)

Rarely does one thing matter. However, when you add a bunch of "one things" together, they can begin to matter quite a bit. This accumulation effect decidedly builds positive or negative momentum.

Think about it this way. Take a dollar out of your wallet. Putting that singular dollar into an investment account kind of seems like a waste of time. What difference is it really going to make? However, if you were to invest a dollar per day, every day, for 45 years, you would have set aside a nest egg of almost $290,000.00. Now we're talking about some real money. That's the power of the cumulative effect (and compounding interest).

This same thing holds true in other areas of our life as well. If we make one negative comment to someone, it likely won't really matter. However, if we make negative comments every day, pretty soon that relationship is going to go south. (This negative momentum is the reason 50% of marriages end in divorce.)

The bottom line is the consistency of our words and actions matter far more than most people would like to admit. They are the fuel of either the positive or negative momentum we are building in our life.

When I first began to wrap my head around Joe's cumulative theory, I only looked at it from the perspective of our actions. I considered how our positive or negative behaviors worked for us or against us. How they could enhance or undermine the life we were trying to build. However, through my reboot, I gained an entirely new and far more powerful perspective on his cumulative theory.

Although our actions certainly build positive or negative momentum for us, our thoughts and beliefs are ultimately the root cause of these actions. I didn't fully appreciate the cumulative nature of my negative thoughts and limiting beliefs, nor did I understand the overwhelming ripple effect they had caused.

Stop and look at the most important areas of your life: What kind of momentum are you building? Where are your decisions and actions leading you? Now, stop and consider the thoughts and beliefs you have locked onto that are driving these actions. Ask yourself, have you been leveraging the cumulative effect to create the life you want or the one you don't want? You have the power to consciously choose one or the other.

The Challenge with Choice

Frankly, if all of our choices about what we wanted to believe were left purely up to us *and* if we were able to make these choice at a time in our life when we had a higher level of wisdom and experience, we would all be much better off.

However, as neurodevelopmental pediatrician Dr. Rajeshree Singhania helped me to understand, most of what we come to believe is defined for us in early adolescence. Once these beliefs are established, they will influence the thoughts that roll through our head for the balance of our lives.

As human beings, we have the longest adolescent development cycle of any species on the planet. In the early phases of this, largely between the ages of 2 and 7, our brain operates almost entirely in an alpha and theta wave state. It is in this brain phase where our mind is most open and impressionable; it records and stores nearly everything it experiences, without filtering or interpreting it. It just accepts what it receives as fact.

Evolution made us this way as a self-defense mechanism to perpetuate the species. The beliefs our ancestors soaked up were about where danger lay and how to find food and shelter. Our ancestors passed down these survival beliefs to their children, generation by generation. To no small extent, this cycle of handing down beliefs is the reason each of us is here today.

However, over time as our world and way of life have changed, so too has the nature of the beliefs that have gotten handed down changed.

Today, the beliefs are less about survival in a danger-laden harsh environment and more about ourselves, our capabilities, and what we can or can't do. Many times, this is where flawed beliefs creep into our subconscious.

It is in this window of time when the foundational programs that make up the operating system of our mind, the optimal programs that we are born with, begin to get reprogrammed and go out of whack. In essence, evolution hands us a fully functioning, perfect software package, and we as human beings inadvertently screw it up. (Hmm, as a species, we certainly have been known to do that before, haven't we?)

Through my journey, I've met tens of thousands of people; unfortunately, very few have the benefit of operating without the influence of limiting beliefs. I know in my own life, everything I have struggled with can be traced back to limiting beliefs and excessively negative thoughts.

As children, these limiting beliefs are thrust on us by the people around us and society as a whole. Unfortunately, it happens to us when our brains are operating in a state where we are powerless to defend again them. It is a sad reality that people with broken brains will automatically perpetuate broken brains in the people around them.

In essence, the choices of what we will believe as adults will largely be made for us as children. We inherit these just like we inherit the color of our eyes and hair. As children, we have no more say in the beliefs we are handed than we do in the shade of our eyes.

Although we are powerless to change our past because the beliefs we were handed are already there and cannot be taken back, remember that our greatest asset in life is our power of choice. We don't have to blindly and unquestioningly accept the limiting beliefs we may have been handed. We can choose what we want to believe as adults; this insight is critical to our ability to reboot our brain.

The Journey Ahead: Making Our Most Important Choices

The good news is that it isn't a million different beliefs that we need to change in order to facilitate our mental reboot and restart our motivational intelligence. In fact, it is just a critical few. In the chapters ahead we will talk about what these are and why making the conscious choice to believe the right things in these areas is so critically important.

As I was reflecting on my rebooting process, I realized that there were two levels of choices we have to make to positively affect our mindset and thus redirect our life in a profoundly better way. The first level of choices relates to our "core beliefs"—think of these like the central operating system of the mind. Without these foundational beliefs in the right place, the operating system of our mind just does not, cannot, work right. When we were born, this mental operating system worked perfectly, just like how your new computer worked perfectly on the first day you brought it home and took it out of the box. However, almost immediately as you begin loading on new programs, new software, the operating system gets corrupted and begins to slow down and not work as efficiently. The same exact thing happens in our mind. As we begin to grow as children, we learn things, embrace messages, and are influenced by those around us. However, not everything we learn helps us; some of it corrupts that central operating system and makes it work less effectively.

In the next three chapters we will restore that mental operating system back to its original, fully functioning, perfect state. With this we will be ready to then rebuild the software programs that cause us to act and react the way that we do.

Next, we will work together to clean up the mental software that shapes our perspectives and drives our happiness and satisfaction in life. This will be the second phase of our rebooting process. In it we will explore the myths and the truths of life.

In working with hundreds of thousands of people over the course of the last three decades, what I learned is that there are eight myths (five fundamental ones and three super myths) that ultimately create the vast majority of our unhappiness, dissatisfaction, and disillusionment with our life. If we can replace these myths with the truths, we liberate ourselves from the ties that bind most people to a life of misery and mediocrity.

India's first female prime minister, Indira Gandhi, once said,

"The power to question is the basis of all human progress."

I ask you to read through each of the following chapters closely. Keep an open mind and answer these questions:

- What is it that you believe?
- How do these beliefs influence the way you move and the choices you make?
- Are these beliefs helping you or hurting you in building the life you most want?
- What is it that you see the people around you believing?
- If you let go of these negative thoughts and limiting beliefs, what do you think your life would look like? What different decisions would you make?

The bottom line is, we can train our brain just like we can train our muscles. Our muscles control our movements. Our mind translates our outside world into happiness or misery.

Make your beliefs a conscious choice and choose wisely; nothing will influence your life more.

PEOPLE–LEADER PERSPECTIVE

Great people leaders understand the importance of coaching and mentoring. It is ultimately one of our highest payoff activities. Much of what makes someone great in this aspect of their role will be their ability to influence the choices of their people. Of these choices, none will matter more than the choice of what they come to think and believe.

In the section ahead, we will discuss the two most important core beliefs that leaders must reinforce within their team. If either of these core beliefs is improperly grounded, it will become exceptionally difficult to drive adaptability, strategy, change, or increased performance within the team.

CHAPTER 7

Rebooting Your Control of You

Earlier in our conversation, we looked at ourselves as children. We looked at how we operated and moved. It was at this point in our life when our brain was working perfectly, without restriction. This was when our mental operating system had no flawed programs, nothing that was holding us back or misshaping our perspective on ourselves. In simple terms, no one had taught us any limiting beliefs. For most of us, me included (at least until our reboot), this was the last time we were really programed to build the life we most want for ourselves.

The goal of our reboot is to reset our mental operating system back to what it was when we were young, before we had been conditioned in negative and limiting ways. To do this we need to reflect on how a child thinks, specifically the way they think prior to the age of two. Why two? Remember, that's when the outside world began to shift the optimal beliefs we were born with.

So, let's take a couple of minutes and look back in the mirror at that young child. Let's reexamine the world through their perspective based on the way they think.

When you get quiet and still, one of the very first things you will notice in young children is that they have absolutely no deflective behaviors. They don't make excuses. They don't rationalize why they can't do something. They don't place blame. Prior to the age of two, children take complete ownership over themselves.

Just consider how differently life would look if a young child was rooted in excuses, blame, and rationalization. Every time they struggled, every time they encountered adversity, every time they fell down, it would prompt an excuse, a rationalization as to why others could walk, and they couldn't. They would default to thoughts like "walking must just come naturally to some people, but not to me," or "this talking stuff is just impossible." Think about it: if children were born with the knowledge that they could make excuses, place blame, and rationalize why every hardship was a reason to stop trying, you and I would look around us and see a world full of adults crawling around babbling incoherent sounds. I guess it is a good thing that children don't make excuses, place blame, or rationalize why they can't succeed.

Now, let's contrast a young child's behavior against what we frequently see in adults. Just look around you. Listen to people speak. You won't have to pay attention for too long before you'll start noticing all the excuses, blame, finger-pointing, and rationalization. It would seem that from the perspective of many adults, virtually everything in their world is outside of their control. It's almost as if they are but powerless pawns destined to have life thrust down up on them.

Just look at the shift in perspective: young children move based upon the belief they are in control, many adults move from the perspective of being an out-of-control victim of their circumstances, environment, and influences. Well, here's the problem with that victim perspective. In life, people with victim mindsets never win. This is a fundamental truth that most people fail to recognize, much to their own undoing.

Excuses, rationalization, blame, and finger-pointing are the foundational cornerstones of a victim mindset. These are the single greatest killers to a life of promise and success. Nothing limits a person more than the thought that *it is someone else's fault, there is nothing they can do,* or that *they are powerless to change things.*

Many years ago, I met a gentleman by the name of Gus Fernandez. I will never forget him imparting these words of advice to me:

"In life, you can make excuses, or you can make yourself successful, but you can't make both."

Certainly, bad things will happen to us. Circumstances will create challenges. People will say and do things that will hurt and disappoint us. At one time or another, in one form or another, these things will happen to everyone. It is the unfortunate reality of life. However, allowing the misfortunes of life to manifest into victim thinking is simply toxic.

BREAKING THE SHACKLES OF VICTIM THINKING

For most of my life (maybe almost all of my life), I lived as a victim. I didn't realize this prior to my reboot. Why? I just didn't have the perspective I needed; I was too close, too immersed in my excuses and blame. They were so much a part of me, guiding me each day, that I couldn't separate myself from them.

One of the greatest gifts of almost dying was it helped me to break away from my bullshit, the lies I had been telling myself and excuses I used to rationalize them. Yes, bad things had happened to me. People had done things that hurt me, disappointed me, and made me feel insignificant. I hadn't always been treated the way I wanted to be, maybe the way I should have been.

So what, big deal, stop whining about it, and step up. Are you going to let the bad things in your past define your future? Are you going to let all the negative that is behind you make everything in front of you negative as well?

Prior to my reboot these were questions I never even considered (so I guess my default answer to these questions was *Yes! I am going to let the bad things in my past define my future. I am going allow the negative that is behind me to make everything in front of me negative as well.*). I didn't even realize I had a choice. I just blindly accepted that my past was destined to define my future (or at the very least significantly influence it).

I think this is true for so many of us. We never separate ourselves from our past negative experiences and really look at how they shape us, how they influence our perspective and undermine the view we have of ourselves and our capabilities. But do they? Do our past negative experiences really have to diminish us, undermine us?

Or, perhaps is it all the bad stuff that fuels the potential within us? Does our negative give us strength, power, and perseverance?

Not only can we rise above our past; if we let it, our past will empower us to build a better future, not only for us but also for all those around us.

I think this was one of, if not the greatest, gift of my reboot. The power to let go, to detach and to control my perspective, rather than be a victim of my past.

Recognizing When Victim Thinking Knocks at the Door

How does someone know when they have stepped into the minefield of victim thinking? The easiest way to tell is just to look and listen. Look at the emotions we are feeling. Are they predominantly negative emotions (fear, anger, disgust, sadness, frustration, resentment, jealousy, and so on)? Next, listen to the little voice we're hearing in our head: Are we comparing ourselves to others? Are we feeling sorry for ourselves? Are we spewing out blame? Are we pointing fingers? Are we making excuses? Are we rationalizing why something won't work? Negative emotions and self-talk are the call signs of victim thinking.

Spending too much time vacillating, pondering, or beating ourselves up over the bad things that happen gets us nowhere. Pointing fingers and making excuses just perpetuates a sense of hopelessness, and this victim mentality only makes us feel out of control and unhappy.

Bad things happen to everyone, not just us. Accept that; it is the truth. Granted, we likely notice the bad things that happen to us more than we notice the bad things that happen to others; however, rest assured, bad things happen to everyone, not just us.

"It's not what happens to you, but how you react to it that matters."

These were the words of the Greek philosopher Epictetus more than 2,000 years ago. What was true then is just as true today. What we choose to think, what we choose to do, and how we choose to react when challenges arise makes all the difference. These choices can empower us to greatness or destine us to mediocrity.

Throughout history there are thousands of examples of great things that have come from very bad situations simply because someone chose to think and react to them differently.

• Jonas Salk invented the polio vaccine because more than half a million people every year were becoming paralyzed and dying from the virus. Out of bad things came something that has saved millions of lives.

- Mary Kay Ash started a billion-dollar company because she was passed over for promotion by her boss. She decided she wanted to control her own destiny and created a company that has helped hundreds of thousands of people to do the same. Out of Mary Kay's "misfortune" came her greatest success.
- John Hetrick invented the airbag in 1953 after being in a severe auto accident with his wife and seven-year-old daughter. Between 1987 and 2017, more than 50,000 lives were saved by this device (airbags didn't become mandatory in automobiles until 1998). Out of John's car crash came his inspiration to help save others.

These are but a few examples of the countless times that people have taken their "bad luck," "misfortune," or "setbacks" and leveraged them as an opportunity to benefit the greater good. The only reason they were able to do so is because they took ownership for their situation, rather than justifying, rationalizing, or making an excuse as to "how bad they have it" or "why negative things always happen to them."

The sad reality is that most of the people we will meet in life will not think this way. Rather, they will have spent a greater portion of their life perfecting their ability to find a reason why something won't work, why it can't be done, or why it is somebody else's fault. They will have become masters of making excuses, rationalizations, and pointing fingers.

However, here is the challenge. Whenever someone makes an excuse, rationalizes why something can't happen, or points a finger at someone else, they have just relinquished all of their power; they have put themselves into a victim mode of thinking. Rest assured; victim thinkers never win. It is impossible.

Why? Because you can't build anything on a foundation of victim thinking. It is a foundation that is no more stable than shifting sand. Victim thinking won't support, can't support, anything of magnitude. Victims never win.

So why are some people able to escape the debilitating grasp of victim thinking while other get mired in it like quicksand?

It all comes down to awareness and choice. People who achieve something of magnitude in life, regardless of circumstance or obstacles, simply have a different, better mindset. It is a mindset that is firmly rooted in two words: ***ultimate responsibility.***

What Is Ultimate Responsibility?

In our life, there is much that we don't have control over. We don't control the weather, the government, the economy, the actions of others . . . (I could go on and on). Certainly, we can have an influence over these things, but don't kid yourself; we don't control them.

In fact, when you really step back and look at it, you and I only have unilateral control over two things in our life (yup, that's right, just two things). What are they?

• We have absolute control over what we choose to pay attention to.
• We have absolute control over the actions we take.

Nothing else in life is completely under our control. When a person truly takes ownership of those two things, they are accepting *ultimate responsibility*.

These two words are perhaps the most empowering words in the English language. These 22 letters, when combined the right way, have the power to dramatically move your life in an incredibly positive direction.

Why is this? For the simple reason that people who accept *ultimate responsibility* relinquish their excuses, their blame, and their rationalizations. They take ownership of what they can control—what they pay attention to and what they do. They don't wallow in self-pity or negative emotions; they just learn from setbacks, make the appropriate adjustments, and try again.

Anybody can point out the problems, anybody can complain about the challenges, and anybody can find an excuse why something won't work. Successful people don't get lost in the problems; they find a way to solve or work around them.

Every child is born firmly rooted in their belief that they are *ultimately responsible*. You were born believing in your *ultimate responsibility*; it is one of the only reasons you can walk and talk today. We must reboot this essential program of our mind if we want to move our life in a better direction. *Ultimate responsibility* is the first essential belief that is required for restarting our motivational intelligence and rebooting our brain.

IF THERE'S A PROBLEM . . .

My mentor's mentor, Randy, lives in Northern California. He is, without question, the wisest person I have ever met. Each time I speak with him, he has this unique ability to create light bulbs that explode in my head as he helps me to see life from a perspective that I didn't even know existed a few minutes before.

About a decade ago, I was working with a client in Northern California, and I reached out to Randy to let him know that I was going to be in town and to see if we could find a time to grab dinner together. We set up a time, and I was looking forward to reconnecting.

On the morning of my trip, I was packing up my suitcase and preparing to head to the airport. As I was getting ready, Michelle and I got into an argument about something or other. So I found myself driving to the airport frustrated and aggravated with her.

I fly to California and have a client meeting that afternoon. That evening, Randy and I are getting together for dinner.

I arrive at the restaurant and sit down with Randy. He looks at me, and with his deep voice he says, "So, David, how are you?"

"I'm doing great, Randy, thanks for asking."

"How are the children doing?" he asks.

"They're doing great, Randy. They're getting so big."

"Yes, they will do that," he replies. "How is Michelle doing?" he asks.

"She's doing great as well, Randy."

"Fantastic. How are the two of you doing?" he asks next.

"Well, we're doing all right," I reply.

(Now, Randy is a great active listener, so he instantly picked up on the fact that I answered that last question differently than I had the ones before, so he immediately homed in on that.)

"What's going on there?" he asks.

So, I proceed to tell him about the argument she and I got into that morning. I said, "It's no big deal, we'll get over it, I'm just a little frustrated with her right now."

Well, I'll never forget what he did next, because he looked me dead square in the eyes and said, "David, if there's a problem, you're the problem. Fix the problem."

Now, between you and me, that wasn't the advice I was looking for that evening. I was all caught up in how she was the problem. However, look what Randy did: he put me right back into a position of *ultimate responsibility*.

(continued)

If there is a problem and I'm not doing anything to fix that problem, then I have just become the problem.

If there is a problem, you're the problem. Fix the problem!

I have reflected quite a bit on these words and have come to realize how much they empower a person in their journey through life.

If there is a problem, if that problem is bothering you, if it is causing you pain, creating negative thinking, distracting you from going in the direction you desire—and you are doing nothing to fix that problem—then **you are the problem**. It is "your" problem—fix the problem and move forward. So, stop complaining and start doing something to make the situation better. Fix the problem!

Taking Ownership of You?

The Swiss-American psychologist Elisabeth Kübler-Ross once said,

"I am in control of me; that is all that matters."

Teddy Roosevelt, America's 26th president, once said,

"If you could kick the person in the pants responsible for most of your troubles, you wouldn't sit for a month."

Benjamin Franklin, the iconic inventor, statesman, and polymath, once said,

"Those who are good for making excuses are seldom good for anything else."

Are you seeing a theme here? Notable icons from differing fields all recognize the same fundamental truth. People who truly understand the concept of *ultimate responsibility* fully embrace these statements. Anytime there is an issue, challenge, or problem, they immediately begin to ask themselves, *What is the best way for me to respond?* They don't waste a nanosecond of their precious life wallowing in self-pity or bemoaning how bad things are.

When my son Ben was 10 years old, we were having a family dinner one night and he made a brilliant observation when he said,

"You really don't have the right to complain if the answer to your problem is right under your fingertips."

Sometimes the most profound observations flow from the mouths of children. The answer to most of our problems, our challenges, our frustrations is almost always right under our fingertips. However, we will only find it when we accept that whatever happened, happened; it is history, it cannot be changed, it cannot be altered, it can only be responded to. What is the best response? That is all that matters.

The good news is, if you want to regain control, there are only three things that you really need to accept *ultimate responsibility* for in life to accomplish everything that you want.

Step 1: Accept Ultimate Responsibility for Your Path

The first area is with regard to the goals that you want to pursue. Only you can decide what success means in your life. Don't get me wrong; advertisers will spend billions each year trying to convince you that driving a certain car, wearing certain clothes, or living a certain lifestyle will make you happy. It won't. The only thing that will make you happy is living life on your own terms, pursuing the goals that you want to pursue. Therefore, don't let others define your path for you; you must accept *ultimate responsibility* here.

Step 2: You Must Accept Ultimate Responsibility for Your Person

The second area where you need to accept ultimate responsibility is for who you need to become in order to accomplish your goals. Most anything that really matters, that will bring real joy into your life, will require you to learn new skills and abilities to achieve it. Great things happen for people who are constantly working to become more, to learn more.

Whenever you're growing, you will feel happy and free of material yearnings. If you're unsatisfied, criticizing yourselves, or feeling hopeless, don't let that stall you out. The easiest way to stay positive is to identify the ways you're making progress as a person, which helps you to see, feel, and appreciate the value of what you're doing.

Step 3: Accept Ultimate Responsibility for Your Perseverance

The third and final thing you must accept *ultimate responsibility* for is the challenges that you will encounter as you pursue your goals. There is no such thing as a perfect plan. Rarely, if ever, will everything go flawlessly. You will not have perfect information. You will be learning things as you go. You will fall down. You will make mistakes. You will encounter resistance. You will have setbacks. Things will take longer than you would like to happen. These are all the realities. When these realities happen, don't waste any mental energy thinking about who or what to blame. Rather, invest your time and energy in figuring out how you are going to persevere and solve the challenge. You and everyone around you will be forever grateful for this *and* you will differentiate yourself from most every other person you will meet in life.

Your Obstacles Form the Foundation of Your Success

Oprah Winfrey was born into abject poverty in a rural Mississippi community. As a child she was repeatedly physically and sexually abused. Told by all around her that she was "no good" and would "never amount to anything," her future looked anything but promising.

Early in her career she took a job working for a radio station and then decided she wanted to work in TV; however, network executives told her she was too ugly to be an on-air personality. Oprah had every reason to fail in life. However, she persevered and today is called the "Queen of all media" and has a net worth of more than $2 billion. Oprah once said,

"I don't think of myself as a poor, deprived ghetto girl who made good. I think of myself as somebody who from an early age knew I was responsible for myself, and that I had to make good."

In the early part of the 2000s, Nick Woodman was a budding tech entrepreneur with a startup that crashed and burned, making no money in the process. Undeterred, he shut down the business and tried his hand with another business idea; this one failed as well. Now having lost more than $4 million and a lot of credibility and confidence, he had to decide what to do next. Should he let go of his entrepreneurial dreams and find a job or try again? He decided on the latter. His third try was the charm. He founded GoPro, and became a billionaire in the process. Nick Woodman once said,

"Nobody likes to fail; you start to question whether your ideas are any good. These are the moments when you dig deep and learn the most about yourself."

Viktor Frankl had earned both his MD and PhD. He was pursuing a promising career in neurology while living in Vienna, Austria. However, with the rise of Nazi Germany, Viktor, his wife, mother, father, and brother were all rounded up and sent to concentration camps. Sadly, none of his family survived.

Viktor spent three years in four different concentration camps struggling to survive. As a man of science and medicine, he took the most horrific aspect of his life and learned from it. After being liberated when the war ended, he went on to lecture around the world, teaching of his experiences, ultimately being nominated for a Nobel Prize for his work. He authored 39 books, the most famous of which, *Man's Search for Meaning*, was voted by the Library of Congress as one of the top 10 most influential books ever written. Viktor Frankl once said,

"The one thing you can never have taken away is your ability to choose how you want to respond. The last of one's freedoms is to choose one's attitude in a given situation."

In each of these incredible success stories, and countless millions of others, you will see that great accomplishments are always built on a foundation of obstacles overcome. Accept *ultimate responsibility* for your challenges, find a way around them, and you will be astonished at what you can achieve.

Take *ultimate responsibility* of these three things:

- Your path (owning where you want to go)
- Your person (owning who you need to become)
- Your perseverance (owning your challenges)

Regardless of what happens, good or bad, you will always be in control of your own destiny.

THE POWER OF WILLINGNESS

One night, I was sitting in a hotel room just relaxing and unwinding after a busy day meeting with a client. As I was flipping through the channels on TV, I stopped off on the A&E Network as they were playing one of my favorite programs, *Biography*. In the series, they pick some notable figure from history and tell that person's story. This particular evening the story was about Haroldson Hunt.

It was 1921, and 32-year-old Haroldson Hunt was flat broke and down on his luck. He had worked as a dishwasher, a farm worker, and a sheep herder. He tried his hand at cotton farming and raising horses. All of these endeavors ended up leaving him further in the hole. To look at his life, you would think, here goes another one of the countless people who are destined to aimlessly wander through life, struggling and never making ends meet.

Yet, this was not to be. In 1974, when Hunt passed away at the ripe old age of 85, he was reputed to be one of the wealthiest people in the world with a net worth of more than $5 billion.

How was he able to do it? How was he able to amass such a great fortune in slightly more than 50 years? How was he able to go from being down on his luck, flat broke, to being a multibillionaire?

On the show that night, they had a clip of an old interview that Hunt had done in the 1960s. The reporter asked Hunt, "If you had to give anyone else advice about how to become successful, what would you tell them?"

Hunt reflected for a moment and shared a very simple formula that he discovered. It was a formula that is as universal as 2 + 2 = 4. A formula that will work for anyone, regardless of who they are or where they are starting from.

Here is the incredible wisdom, the formula for success that Haroldson Hunt shared in his reply to that reporter.

"The secret to success is really relatively easy; you just need to do two things. First, you need to decide exactly what it is you want to achieve, and then second, you must willingly pay the dues to go and get it."

However, he also said,

"The problem that most people have is that they don't really know what they want to achieve, and even if they do, they're not willing to pay the dues to go and get it."

I remember watching that episode like it was yesterday. As I reflect on Hunt's words, it is abundantly clear the reason why he was so successful: he accepted *ultimate responsibility* for the goals he wanted to pursue and for who he needed to become to accomplish them.

Rest assured, it was not luck, circumstances, or some outside factor that made Hunt a billionaire. It was his willingness to accept *ultimate responsibility* for what truly mattered.

Shifting Our Perspective on Control

From an early age we are immersed in a culture of excuse making and rationalization. Children, as master observers, notice this behavior in adults and begin to model it from a remarkably young age. Noted Yale child psychologist William Kessen observed blame-shifting behaviors in children as young as four years old. In simple terms, most people have been practicing making excuses almost as long as they have been practicing walking. As such, this behavior comes as easily, as naturally, as walking does for most of us. It takes virtually no effort, no energy, and no thought to come up with an excuse or rationalization as to why something can't be done.

So how are we to break a long-held habit pattern that comes so easily? How can we escape a debilitating behavior that is so engrained? These are extremely valid and important questions.

To find answers and to once and for all liberate ourselves, we must reflect back on the two things we have absolute control over in life:

- What we pay attention to
- The actions that we take

Within these two items exists the key that will unshackle us from victim thinking and once again enable us to regain control over our life.

Anytime someone is dwelling on the negative, ruminating on the bad aspects, or getting lost in how something has been taken away from them—their brain will automatically default into victimized-excuse mode, blame will flow, and rationalizations will abound. They have lost their sense of control. A feeling of powerlessness and a groundswell of negative emotions will not be far behind.

When someone is living with *ultimate responsibility*, it's not that they ignore, deny, or turn a blind eye to life's negative twists and turns. There will always be struggles and suffering, sometimes more and sometimes less; these things will always be present and with us. Taking a Pollyanna, devil-may-care approach will not change things nor make anything in any way better.

Rather, accepting *ultimate responsibility* means we acknowledge the reality of the situation, good or bad, positive or negative, and instead of dwelling on the hardship, we consider what is our best response and look for options rather than excuses. Victims immerse themselves in the pain. People who accept *ultimate responsibility* immerse themselves in their response. This is no small difference. One depowers, the other empowers.

There are two simple questions we can ask ourselves that will dramatically help us to make this important mental shift.

Question 1: What Exactly Is the Problem?

Most people's brains are inherently conditioned to go looking for an excuse, someone to blame, or a rationalization as to why they can't succeed as soon as a hardship presents itself. It is a well-engrained mental pattern. However, it's also a pattern we can override and eventually replace, if we just condition ourselves to ask a better question.

Asking ourselves, "What exactly is the problem?" forces us to seek to understand, first. Take the time to really consider your response here. What are the underlying issues that make this a problem (key consideration: how many of them are internal to you versus externally driven)? What is the root cause of this problem (key insight: many times our best insights will come from taking the time to understand the problem behind the problem)?

Once we really understand the nature of the problem, we are ready to ask ourselves the second question.

Question 2: What Can I Do About the Problem?

What is your best response or way to react to this problem? Consider your options: what will the cause and effect be for each? Will a given response move you closer to where you want to be or further away? Will your intended response improve the situation, keep it the same, or make it worse?

Recognize that you don't always have perfect information, so even after careful consideration, you may not know the full ripple effect of your response. That's okay and shouldn't be used as an excuse for doing nothing. Worst-case scenario, action creates information and information enables us to make better decisions moving forward. Author Matt Armstrong once said,

"The most dangerous risk in life is to risk nothing."

Remember that you are not powerless; there is always something that you can do. Even if it's just to accept the problem, change your attitude about it and deal with it.

Stand Up and Take Control

Don't wait for life to come to you, don't wait for others to do things for you, don't wait for people to make you happy. Don't wait till the last minute, don't wait to be given something. Stand up, take control. Life will never deliver to you anything but sadness, disappointment, and despair if you sit idly by waiting for someone else to make you happy or for someone to give you something to make your life better. This is what I learned through my reboot and what I want to pass on to you.

The world is full of people who will stand and wait. Hoping, wishing, dreaming of winning the lottery, having the perfect person stumble into their life, becoming an overnight success. However, waiting and wishing is a lousy strategy for finding happiness and success. They don't make shoes that are comfortable enough to stand and wait that long for these things to happen. You must make them happen. You must take control of your own destiny.

Ultimate responsibility is the first fundamental program of your newly rebooted brain. Embrace it, and it will forever serve you well.

PEOPLE–LEADER PERSPECTIVE

Any leader can attest to the cancerous effect of excuse making, finger-pointing, blame, and rationalization. These negative behaviors frequently run rampant within organizations and create much of the resistance that leaders experience every day.

Breaking the victim mentality and fostering a culture rooted in *ultimate responsibility* is the first fundamental step a leader must focus on to move a team in a more productive direction.

In our conversation moving forward we will explore different proven strategies and techniques to help you breathe life into this critical belief.

CHAPTER 8

Rebooting Your Limitless Ability to Learn

Do you have the ability to learn?

It's a seemingly simple question that most people will inherently say yes to without really giving it a second thought. Sure, we can all learn things. However, how far does your ability to learn extend? Does it only apply to learning simple and easy things, or does it apply to anything and everything we could think of?

Could you, for instance, learn to play the guitar or piano? Could you learn about macroeconomics, monetary policy, and the underpinnings of what drives inflation? Could you learn about quantum mechanics, string theory, and muons? Could you learn about molecular biology, gene-splicing, and how to edit DNA using CRISPR?

Could you learn enough about any of these things to become an expert in them? Could you become world-renowned for your knowledge and share it on conference stages across the globe?

Perhaps it's not so easy to say yes anymore. Certainly, we believe that others can learn these things, but what about us?

When you get quiet and still, what do you really believe about your ability to learn: does it have limits? Are there boundaries to your capability to absorb new knowledge?

Sure, we may not have the desire to learn about things. Perhaps it is our lack of interest that is stopping us. Or maybe, just maybe, that's an excuse we use to hide a limiting belief.

As I was going through my reboot, I realized how giving up our control by making excuses, placing blame, and rationalizing why things couldn't or wouldn't work out absolutely undermined my happiness, satisfaction, and ability to live my life on more optimal terms. In essence, I frequently gave away my control and with it any opportunity to find peace of mind.

The first belief we must reset to reboot our brain is *ultimate responsibility*. With this belief properly back in place (where it was when we were small children), we are once again in control of our destiny.

The challenge is, believing in our own *ultimate responsibility* isn't enough. Yes, it is a critical first step. However, there is one other program of the mind that we must also reset to start our rebooting process.

So, let's once again go back to the beginning of our story. Let's revisit that little boy, that little girl, as they are crawling across the floor. What other essential life lesson can they teach us about ourselves? What other beliefs were driving them to move the way that they did?

Reflect back and remember how many times we fell down in that process of learning to walk. About 17 times an hour, right? That meant we were falling about every three minutes. Imagine falling forward, backward, sideways, hitting your head, butt, elbows, or hands on the ground every three minutes for months on end and never giving up, never doubting yourself, never second-guessing your ability to learn. Why do children do this? Why did we do it?

We did it for one incredibly important reason. As children we all had an unwavering belief in our *limitless ability to learn*. We placed no boundaries on our capacity to learn. When we were young children, deep in our soul, we knew we could learn how to walk (and, frankly, that belief was reinforced by everyone around us). Sadly, as we get older, often that belief in our *limitless ability to learn* not only wanes in our mind but also stops being reinforced by those around us.

The second major shift that happens in our belief system is when the people around us—our parents, peers, and society at large—begin to teach us that our ability to learn is *limited* rather that *limitless*. It is a subtle reconditioning process that happens because people start comparing us to others.

Sure, we all have the unlimited ability to learn to walk and talk, but parents point out that Billy seems to be better at reading or math. Sally is better at spelling or writing than we are. Slowly a message begins to get sent that others can learn things better than we can. These comparisons plant the seed of doubt regarding our ability to learn.

We just start thinking: it must come more easily to those other people; perhaps they just have innate abilities that we don't have, and right then and there we begin to buy into the belief that our ability to learn must have some limits to it. But does it really? Or is this just a self-perpetuating myth that is handed from one generation to another?

Consider how different life would look if we let go of the myth and regained our belief in our *limitless ability to learn*. We wouldn't need to fear the prospect of change because we would know deep down that no matter what life threw at us, we could learn, adjust, and adapt. We wouldn't need to feel defensive when someone was giving us feedback or telling us that we screwed something up. Why? Because we would recognize that even the harshest critic could provide us with insights we could use to become better, stronger, and more adept.

If we really believed in our *limitless ability to learn*, we would be willing to take greater risks, try bigger things, challenge ourselves more. Why? All for the simple reason that if we knew our downside was limited, our *limitless ability to learn* would provide us with the ability to pivot and always find a way to drive positive outcomes. Suddenly the prospect of making a mistake wouldn't seem so daunting. We wouldn't need to feel the oppressive fear of failure.

Stop! Just think about this next point for a second. Really consider it.

What would you do, what challenges would you undertake, what would you pursue—if you knew it was impossible for you to fail?

Really consider this question for a few moments. I'll wait.

Regaining our belief in our *limitless ability to learn* is the root of our confidence and the source of our courage. It gives us the faith to stand up in the face of uncertainty and the resilience to rebound from setbacks. Michael Gelb, a Batten Institute research fellow at the University of Virginia who has extensively studied our ability to learn, once said,

"Research shows that you begin learning in the womb and go right on learning until the moment you pass on. Your brain has a capacity for learning that is virtually limitless, which makes every person a potential genius."

It was Stanford University psychology professor Dr. Carol Dweck who really helped me understand the importance of making this critical shift in our beliefs about our *limitless ability to learn*.

Earlier in our conversation, we talked about our motivational intelligence. If you remember back, our MQ is our awareness of and ability to manage negative thinking and self-limiting beliefs. What Carol discovered is that people operate under one of two MQ mindsets.

The first is what is called a *fixed mindset*. People with fixed mindsets are more ruled by their negative thoughts and self-limiting beliefs. Put simply, they believe that life is largely outside of their control and that their ability to learn is limited.

So, what's the ripple effect of these limiting beliefs? Really a quite profound one. People with fixed mindsets will tend be more defensive, close-minded, and resistant to change. They often will avoid situations that require them to get outside of their comfort zones and learn new skills and abilities. They won't seek out advice from others and frequently won't listen when it is offered to them. If they try something new and aren't very quickly successful at it, they will give up and move back to the ways they have always done things. Basically, their fixed mindset, their negative thoughts and limiting beliefs, keeps them fixed in place.

The second MQ mindset Carol discovered was what she called a *growth mindset*. People with growth mindsets can still have some negative thinking and self-limiting beliefs (everybody does); however, they are better able to override these internal obstacles. As such, they believe that they have a greater measure of control (or at least the ability to have influence), and they believe in their *limitless ability to learn*.

You will see profoundly different behaviors from someone with a growth mindset. They are open-minded and excited to learn new things. They will actively seek out advice and insights from others. They will keep practicing something until they get good at it. If they make a mistake, they will learn from it and adjust their approach as they try again. (To put it simply, these people still move with the mindset that we all possessed prior to the age of two.)

One of the other insights Carol shared was the fact that it is entirely possible for a person to have a fixed mindset in one area of their life (this will be an area of their life where they are struggling) and a growth mindset in another (this will be an area where they are realizing greater success).

Stop and think about that for a second. Haven't we all seen someone who is excelling in one area of their life and struggling in another? So frequently, it is abundantly clear to us why they are struggling. Yet for whatever reason, they just can't see it. It is like they have blinders on; they just keep making the same mistakes over and over and never learn. Their fixed mindset keeps them in a downward spiral that they just can't seem to pull out of. All because they have locked into a limiting belief in this particular area of their life.

Ultimate responsibility and *limitless ability to learn* are the two beliefs that unlock our motivational intelligence and enable us to reboot our brain. These beliefs guide our perspective, our interpretation, and our responses to everything in life. If one or both are out of whack, a person's life will look dramatically different. Their choices and behaviors will be self-limiting and they will always struggle with the dynamic nature of life.

ACCEPTING ANNICA

Through the course of our lifetime, we will learn to do tens of thousands of things. However, the very first thing we will learn after we are born is to breathe. (This was an interesting little fact that Michelle shared with me one day—she's a labor and delivery nurse who has delivered thousands of babies, so I consider her a credible expert on the subject.)

Once we learn to take our first breath, we will repeat this cycle about every four seconds for the rest of our lifetime. That amounts to about 7 million breaths each year and about 500 million over the course of an average lifetime.

We can live for about 30 days without food and about 4 days without water. We can only live for about 4 minutes without air. Breathing is the most essential and fundamental aspect of our existence.

Prior to COVID, I took breathing for granted. I think most of us do. We seem to take almost everything for granted until we no longer have it, then suddenly we appreciate more what we have lost.

It was Richard Wiseman, professor of psychology at the United Kingdom's University of Hertfordshire, who helped me understand why we do this. He explained that the human brain was programmed by evolution to

(continued)

look for change. (It's another one of the self-defense mechanisms that kept our ancestors alive. Changes oftentimes represented threats, so our ancestors needed to notice changes to protect themselves.)

Richard explained that our brain still works this way. He said, "Think about it. When you walk into the kitchen, you smell the coffee brewing, five minutes later you don't notice it. We pick up on the change in smell when we entered the room. Once we get used to it, we stop noticing it. When things in our life stay the same, our brain stops noticing them, we take them for granted because our brain assumes they will always be the same."

However, things rarely stay the same forever. It was the Buddhist monk Yongey Mingyur Rinpoche who taught me about Annica. It's a Pali word that speaks to the impermanent nature of life. Nothing is constant and everything is always in a state of change. This is a central principle of both Buddhism and Hinduism.

As humans we long for certainty, consistency, and permanence. We don't really like it when things change, take a different direction, or turn out in some unexpected way. However, all too frequently, what we want or like and the way our life turns out are totally unrelated.

Lying in a hospital bed struggling to breathe and feeling weaker by the day, I no longer took the simple act of breathing for granted. I could no longer take any aspect of my life for granted. I realized for the first time in my life that everything is impermanent. Everything is in a constant state of change and not always in a good way.

The pastor Charles Swindoll once said,

"Life is 10% what happens to you and 90% how you choose to react to it."

We don't always get to choose what happens to us in our life; however, when we lock onto the proper beliefs about our own *ultimate responsibility* and *limitless ability to learn,* we recognize that we can always adjust and adapt. As such, no matter what happens to us, at least we get to choose the best response to the changing aspects of our life.

Adversities Will Always Arise and Problems Will Always Present Themselves

Every day, problems, challenges, and obstacles will present themselves to us. They will come in many forms. Some will present themselves overtly, like a car accident or injury. Some will present themselves more subtly, like a tough work assignment or someone being mean to us.

Whether overt or subtle, every challenge, every problem, every obstacle offers us a powerful lesson. It offers a chance to see something and learn something about ourselves and the world. If we approach these challenges with the right mindset, we look for these lessons and they will teach us much of what we will need to know in life.

The author Phyllis Theroux once said,

"Mistakes are the bridge between inexperience and wisdom."

Everything that has happened to us, every success, every misfortune, every triumph, and every heartache has happened for a reason. They are our life lessons, and they exist to teach us something, to help us see or understand something.

Too many people waste a lot of time dwelling on the negative aspects and emotions that come from these misfortunes, which only fosters and reinforces their self-limiting beliefs. Look for the lessons and let them carry you forward; then let go of the pain of the misfortune. It has no further ability to serve you.

When we take a moment periodically throughout each day to stop, get still, think, and reflect, we find these lessons contained within every one of our successes. We find these lessons in every setback. We will find these lessons in our frustrations and challenges. All we have to do is look for them. Ask ourselves, what is this situation trying to teach me? How can I leverage it to make myself better, stronger, smarter, or more resilient? The answers are right in front of us; we just have to be open-minded enough to see and embrace them.

Life has a very funny way of repeating itself. If we don't see the lessons and learn from them, we will repeat the behaviors and find ourselves in the same pattern again. This process will keep repeating until we learn. So many people never see this and end up in a never-ending vortex or cycle of mistakes, discontentment, and struggle.

Shifting Our Perspective on Learning

So how does one break away from a limiting belief about their ability to learn? How do we regain the open-mindedness and adaptability of our youth? These are both pivotal questions that in their answer have the ability to transform our life.

University College London's cognitive neuroscientist Steven Fleming helped me to understand that the human mind is wired for reflection. It has been a central part of cognitive function of our solver/critical brain for close to 4 million years. However, the way we reflect markedly changes as we get older.

When young, our reflection focuses on our actions and how we can adjust them to improve our outcomes. When a toddler falls to the left, they reflect, learn, and adjust such that the next time they stand, they lean more to the right. That little boy or girl wastes no mental energy beating themselves up, second-guessing their capabilities, or justifying why they can't succeed. They just reflect, learn, adjust, and adapt.

As adults, the focus of our reflection becomes less about our actions and how to adapt and more about judging our self-worth. For most people, when they make a mistake, when they screw something up or when things don't turn out the way they would have liked—the first thing they do is judge and criticize themselves based on their mistakes, all the while undermining their sense of self-worth. This is our critical/solver brain creating a negative loop in the mind.

If we want to regain our self-confidence and belief in our ability to learn, we must break that negative loop and reprogram the way we reflect. **Catch this: changing the way we reflect is absolutely essential for rebooting our brain.**

IS YOUR HARSHEST CRITIC YOU?

I had spent two weeks preparing to make my very first sales call. I had learned my hour-long sales presentation frontwards and backwards, practicing it over and over until I could virtually do it in my sleep. I practiced that presentation on my mom and dad, I did it again and again for Michelle. Heck, I even did that presentation for our dog because she would lie there for an hour and pretend to listen.

I was feeling confident and ready to go out and run my first live sales meeting. My sales manager offered to ride along with me for moral support and to help coach me afterwards. So, we drove together to the appointment, and as we neared our destination, I could feel my heart start to beat faster. My breathing got shallower, and I began to get cold sweats. It felt like I was on the verge of a full-on panic attack.

In my mind, I kept telling myself, "Dave, you got this, you know the presentation, it's only an hour, you'll do fine." Meanwhile, I'm trying to look like I've got my shit together in front of my sales manager sitting next to me in the car. I was a wreck.

We get out of the car and walk into the office building. The receptionist takes us to the office of the guy I am supposed to be meeting with. I reach out and shake his hand, sit down, and launch into my sales presentation (please do notice the operative word I used there—*launch*).

I launched into this presentation like a high-speed bullet train. I've got words coming out of my mouth like bullets coming out of a machine gun. Yet, I'm so nervous, I don't even realize I'm doing it. I'm just on autopilot.

Finally, I run out of words, so I stop, take a breath, and really look at the guy sitting on the other side of the desk from me. Here's what I remember. His hair was plastered back, his eyes were watering, and he had a death grip on the arms of his chair. He looked like a tornado had just ripped through his office with him sitting there. I can assure you, that guy never had anyone have a full-on category 5 meltdown right in front of him like what he just witnessed.

So, there were no sales made that day. We get up to leave, and as I'm walking out of his office, I glanced down at my watch. And I notice that exactly 17 minutes had passed since we had walked in. (Yup, that's right, I had condensed an entire 60-minute presentation down to a 17-minute window of time.)

Then, like a freight train it hits me, I just royally f&@ked up. All my negative self-talk starts up. My critical brain goes into overdrive with a litany of undermining statements: "Dave, you can't do this; this isn't the right career path for you; you've got to find something else; what makes you think you can do this, you're an introvert for cripe's sake, this is a job for an extrovert . . ." In a mere flash of seconds, I was ready to give up on myself and quit.

As we stepped on to the elevator, my sales manager smiles, looks at me, and says, "Well, Dave, I just have three questions for you."

Of course, my mind immediately defaults to the negative, so I'm thinking she is going to ask me, "Is your resume up-to-date? Do you have cab fare to get you home? Do you have any experience flipping burgers because that's what I think your next career move should be?" You know, questions like that.

Instead, she just calmly looks at me and asks,

"What did you do right in there?"

(*continued*)

My immediate thought was, "What the f&@k . . . were you in there? I didn't do anything right. That sucked, I sucked, and I quit."

I think she must have sensed my tidal wave of negativity because before I could even open my mouth, she just said, "Take a deep breath, calm down; there were a lot of things you did right in there."

I looked at her flabbergasted and said, "Like what, name *one* thing I did right in there?"

She said, "How about this? I'll name one thing and then you name one thing."

I just rolled my eyes, shook my head, and said, "Okay, name one thing I did right."

She smiled and said, "Well, let's see, I'm pretty sure you kept breathing the whole time."

I couldn't help but laugh at this. "Yeah, I guess I did."

"Now you tell me one thing you did right."

I thought about it for a second and said, "Well, I'm not positive, but I think I got the whole sales presentation in."

She laughed at that and said, "Yes, you did, and I was damn impressed by that. In fact I don't think you missed a single word of that presentation. I don't know if your recognize it or not, but you've got quite a good memory." Then she said, "My second question is,

"What did you do wrong in there?"

I could have written a book in response to that one (well, I guess I kind of am, LOL). I thought about it for a second and replied, "I think I might have rushed it a little bit."

She laughed and said, "Yeah, you were a little quick. My third question is,

"What are you going to do differently next time you run that presentation so that you can be even more effective?"

I kind of smiled at the thought that she was implying that I was at all effective in this first round. And I struggled to come up with an answer.

She said, "Let me help you with that one. Next time you run that presentation, do you think you could focus on sucking a little more air out of the room instead of blowing it all in by talking a million words a minute?"

I started laughing and said, "Yeah, I think I can do that."

She said, "Just slow it down, have fun with it, and you'll do great. Remember, I believe in you."

Although it would take many years and a near-death experience to fully realize it, that day, I learned one of the most important lessons of my entire life. I learned how to stop judging myself and give myself permission to learn from my mistakes. With three simple questions, she showed me how to break feedback away from my sense of self-worth and use it as a learning tool instead of a judgment weapon. What an incredible gift.

Reflecting on How We Are Reflecting

Where have you learned the most in life: from your setbacks or from your successes? For most of us, our setbacks are our best teachers. They offer us a perspective on what not to do, what didn't work out, and what direction we should focus on to make improvements. However, we only gain this insight if we let go of the judgment and begin to learn from our mistakes.

So, how do we break away from the destructive judgment cycle? Great question, I'm glad you asked it. It all starts by changing the way we reflect.

For many adults, reflection begins and ends with just one question:

What did I do wrong?

Their response to this question provides them with all the ammo they need to beat themselves up and convince themselves to quit trying.

A better question to begin reflection with is this:

What did I do right in that situation?

Just asking this as our first question as we come out of difficult situations breaks our existing mental pattern and begins a reprogramming process in our brain. This is absolutely critical for our reboot.

The beautiful thing is, even in our most colossal of screwups, our biggest of catastrophes, or our greatest of meltdowns—there is always something that we did right. Even if that something is just the fact that we had the courage to show up, or that we didn't wet our pants in the middle of it. Face it: if we look hard enough, there are aways a few positive things we did even in the worst of situations. Finding these helps us to feel a little better about ourselves and slows down the mental flogging.

Next, ask yourself: What did I do wrong in that situation?

However, don't waste time with negative emotions or feeling bad about yourself. Just look at your actions. What actions did you take that didn't work? Did you say or do something that fostered a negative outcome. Did you avoid doing something that you should have done? Look for the lessons, not the judgment.

The most important question of all is this: What will I do differently next time to be even more successful?

With this final question, we seal the deal and make everything about learning. Stop and consider it for a second. If we have learned something, gained an insight, or in some way improved our approach for next time—*haven't we been successful?* Sure, we may not have gotten 100% of what we desired at the outset, but at least we made a positive step toward next time. That is a good thing.

- What did I do right in that situation?
- What did I do wrong in that situation?
- What will I do differently next time to be even more successful?

These are the three most important question we will ever ask ourselves in life. With these three questions, we can take the shackles off ourselves and bring ourselves back to the *limitless ability to learn* mindset we were born with.

The beautiful thing is, there is no shortage of places where we can ask these three questions of ourselves. We can use them at work, in our finances, in our relationships, and with regard to our health.

If every day as we approach those important aspects of our life, we are improving, making progress, and moving in the direction we want in life, in time we will get there, and what more could we ask for?

Limitless ability to learn is the second foundational program of your newly rebooted brain. Embrace this belief and you will be forever grateful.

PEOPLE–LEADER PERSPECTIVE

Ultimate responsibility is the first foundational cornerstone of any high-performing team culture. The *limitless ability to learn* is the second foundational cornerstone.

These two beliefs remove the biggest barriers that hold people and teams back in life. *Ultimate responsibility* puts them back in control (thus breaking the victim mindset), the *limitless ability to learn* reminds them of their ability to adjust and adapt. If someone believes they are in control and have the ability to adapt, they no longer need to feel afraid.

Ultimate responsibility and the *limitless ability to learn* are the two core beliefs that are foundational to a person's motivational intelligence. If either of these beliefs is not properly in place, a person will move with a fixed mindset.

CHAPTER 9

Rebooting Your Thought Process

Within our body we have 7 octillion atoms that merge together to create the 3 billion base pairs of DNA that make us uniquely us. These pairs of DNA have built us into a truly magnificent marvel of science.

They have laid the foundation for a structural system of 206 bones and 230 movable joints. Around these bones flows a network of 100,000 miles of vessels that feed blood, oxygen, and nutrients to the 650 muscles that enable our every movement. Around these muscles runs nearly 90,000 miles of nerves. Feeding information into these nerves, we have eyes capable of distinguishing more than 10 million colors, a nose than can remember more than 50,000 scents, and ears that detect changes in the pressure waves of air by moving less than a billionth of an inch so that we can hear.

However, for all the wondrous things that our body does, by far, the most fantastic and incredible aspect of us floats between our ears. A 3-pound organ that, if it were a computer, could perform 38,000 trillion operations per second. By comparison, the world's most powerful supercomputer can manage only .002% of that.

Through this mind will bounce roughly 60,000 conscious thoughts each and every day. Over time, these thoughts will come to define every aspect of who we will become, what we will pursue, and what we will avoid. These thoughts will build on the mental foundation that evolution gave us and shape the way we perceive and react to our world.

More than 2,000 years ago, Gautama Buddha said,

"Our life is shaped by our mind, for we become what we think."

Our thoughts are the most powerful thing that we can influence. Why? For the simple reason that our dominant thoughts are what will shape our future beliefs. These beliefs will define every aspect of our life.

Sadly, most people never accept *ultimate responsibility* for influencing their thoughts in a positive way, thus they allow them to be random: some positive, most negative, some empowering, and many depowering. These random thoughts do little other than confine a person to a life of mediocrity.

THE BACKGROUND NOISE OF OUR MIND

Sit still for a few moments and really stop and listen to all the sounds that you hear around you. Perhaps you hear traffic noise or people moving about; you might hear birds chirping, a dog barking, or the wind rustling. Every day these sounds come and go, they ebb and flow, some louder than others, yet they are always there, and we are immersed in them.

Certainly, we can influence the sounds we hear by clapping our hands, speaking out loud, or turning on some music; however, even if we do nothing, the sounds of our environment will always be there. They are like a soundtrack track in a movie. They underscore our lives and, for most of us, we hear them but hardly give them much attention until we really stop, get still, and listen to them. These external sounds are always there and always present.

Until we accept *ultimate responsibility* for influencing them, in many ways our thoughts will work very much the same way as the background sounds in our outside environment. They are with us every day, flowing through our brain, narrating our life, judging, critiquing, and warning. Sometimes they are soft-spoken and gentle, other times they are angry and full of force. However, one thing they never are is completely silent.

Prior to my reboot, I paid little attention to my thoughts; they were like a companion that was always with me. Sometimes they said shockingly horrible things, making nasty comments about me or other people. My thoughts would mock me, belittle me, or second-guess my decisions. They would place doubts right before I had to do something important, or they would remind me of my past failings if I was thinking of trying something new. As I reflect back now, in many ways my thoughts were not a friend who was encouraging me to be better, smarter, or happier. No, my thoughts were more of an antagonist who was always striving to hold me back.

In 2014, TV journalist Dan Harris released his book, *Ten Percent Happier*. He once told me his original working title for the book was, *The Voice in My Head Is an Asshole*. I still laugh when I think of this, likely because I fully agree with his assessment.

If left to its own devices, our mind likes to write horror stories. It is drawn to the negative and will focus on it, dwelling, mulling, and ruminating on the bad things. In studies, the National Science Foundation discovered that 65–85% of our thoughts lean toward the negative. This negativity is the left-over vestige of our ancestors. Their negative thinking kept them out of harm's way, so they were able to live another day. Our negative thinking just keeps us unhappily treading water in the sea of mediocrity.

Why Are Our Thoughts So Powerful?

I asked this question of my mentor nearly two and a half decades ago. I've never forgotten what he shared in response. Here is what he helped me to understand.

There are two aspects of our mind that play a critical role in our success. Understanding how they work and, most important, how to leverage them, will make an incredible difference in the life we will build for ourselves.

First, is our *conscious mind*. This is where our thoughts live, so it is the aspect of our mind we are most familiar with. Our conscious mind is where we live every waking hour. It is where the voice we hear when we talk to ourselves lives. (Yes, it's not just you, everybody does it. As long as you aren't hearing many different little voices up there, you're all right.)

It's also in our conscious mind that we make decisions, hundreds on hundreds of decisions every day. Everything from the clothes we want to wear today to broader things like what we want to do for a living, or do we want to get married and have kids. In our conscious mind we decide what we want to do. Yet far more important, we must influence our conscious mind in a way that decides what we want to think. Søren Kierkegaard, a man many consider to be the world's first truly existential philosopher, once said,

"Our life always expresses the results of our dominant thoughts."

In its purest and simplest sense, our conscious mind defines the goals and direction of our life. If our conscious mind didn't work this way, the human race would never have survived as a species.

The second aspect of our mind is responsible for developing and executing on the direction given by our conscious mind. It's called our *subconscious mind*. Think of your subconscious mind like an architect there to design the blueprint for building our dominant conscious thoughts into reality. Our subconscious mind doesn't develop these plans independently; it is ruled, governed, and solely directed based on our conscious thoughts.

How does our subconscious develop these plans, the plans to manifest our conscious thoughts into reality? This is one of the most wondrous aspects of us.

Within our subconscious mind, we have recorded and stored everything we have experienced since we were children. Every sight, every sound, every smell, everything we have touched and tasted has been recorded and stored within the deep confines of our subconscious mind.

I was curious about our subconscious memory: How much can we really store, is it limitless, or does it have a maximum capacity like the hard drive on our computer? As I began to research the topic, I was introduced to Dr. Paul Reber, who is a cognitive neuroscientist at Northwestern University and heads their brain, behavior, and cognition research program. He and his team have extensively studied the nature of our memory. I thought he was the perfect person to ask.

He explained that right now they haven't found a defined limit to our memory capacity; however, they do know that we have at least 2.5 petabytes of storage space. (For reference, with that much storage space you could record about 3 million hours of TV programs—that's 300 years' worth of recording).

So, our subconscious mind is indeed a vast library, a huge databank of all our past experiences. Every day that library grows as we keep adding more information and more experiences. Everything we do, everything we learn, every mistake we make adds to our reference points, insights, and knowledge. We use this to refine our existing plans and create the basis for new ones.

So, once we begin to consistently focus on something, once we make something a dominant thought in the forefront of our conscious mind, our subconscious locks on and automatically goes into our data-bank of past experiences looking for those that align or relate. It will take these past experiences and insights and begin to form them into a plan or blueprint to manifest this thought into your reality.

We will go through this process, hundreds if not thousands of times each day. Thinking about something and then executing on it. This is what happens from the moment we wake up and think about getting out of bed.

Creating a New and Better Plan

What about when we are just learning something new, when we are doing something for the first time. How does our brain work then? Another great question that I'm glad you asked.

Anytime we don't have a preexisting pattern or mental plan, our mind works the same way but just with less information to go on. So it will still look to see if you have any insights that even remotely align with your desired new direction. From these insights it will assemble a partial plan. Think of it like a blueprint but with pieces missing, like puzzle pieces that aren't there.

Say, for example, you decided you wanted to learn how to play the guitar. You may have never held a guitar before in your life, but that doesn't mean you know absolutely nothing about playing a guitar. Think about it: you've watched other people doing it, so you do know some things.

From watching others, you have a rough idea how to hold a guitar. You know that with one hand you strum the strings and with the other you move your fingers around to make notes. You don't know how to do either of those things, but you've picked up this much from watching others. Thus, your subconscious can build a rough plan just based on past information gained through watching others.

Next comes the really important part. Anytime your subconscious doesn't have enough internal data to make a complete plan it is trained to go looking externally for more data. Remember our old friend Sir Isaac Newton? Here's where he comes into play, he taught us:

"For every action, there is an equal and opposite reaction."

So, every time we do something, we get a reaction, we'll call that reaction *feedback*.

Our subconscious takes in that feedback from our actions, it studies it, analyzes it, and uses it to fill in those missing pieces of the mental blueprint. The key to getting better at anything is practice. Why? Because practice creates feedback, and feedback is the fuel our subconscious uses to create a new or better mental plan.

Now catch this part; it is really important. Following along with our example from before, when you first pick up that guitar and strum those strings, when you first try moving your fingers around to make musical notes, do you realistically think you'll do it perfectly the first time (or even the 50th time)? No, of course not; you're just learning. You're going to make mistakes, it is going to be awkward and uncomfortable, everybody sucks in the beginning. As such, the feedback you'll be getting will be odd sounds and buzzing strings. The feedback isn't going to be pretty; it isn't going to sound great *but* your subconscious mind doesn't care; it just needs the feedback. The more of it that it can get and the faster it can get it, the better. Feedback is what builds our mental plans.

This is an incredibly important point that we will circle back to later in our conversation. In the early phases of learning anything, you are going to make mistakes, things aren't going to work out well, it is going to feel awkward and uncomfortable; as a result, you are going to want to quit and move on to something easier. However, recognize all the feedback you're getting from those mistakes and those screwups is being taken in by your subconscious mind and used to hone and refine your mental plan. Each time you botch something up, it helps your subconscious mind adjust and refine. It's no different from each time you fell down as a child. Every stumble got you one step closer to walking. The great author and playwright Fay Weldon once said,

"Only one thing registers in the subconscious mind: repetitive application—practice. What you practice is what you manifest."

Remember, anytime you see anyone who is really great at doing something, all you're watching is someone who gave themselves permission to spend a lot of time practicing;' thus, they took in a great deal of feedback in that area of their life. All that feedback enabled them to build a master level plan for doing what you are now watching them do flawlessly.

Living Our Life According to Our Plans

On the day that you and I were born, we had no mental plans, we hadn't yet learned to do anything, our subconscious mind was a blank slate. As a newborn, we hadn't even learned how to breathe yet. However, within seconds of us coming into this world, our subconscious mind began to learn, and it began creating the plans necessary for us to live. First, we developed a plan for breathing, next we developed a plan for eating. These were the first things our subconscious had to learn in order for us to survive.

As we grew older, our dominant thoughts began to kick in, and we began to consciously choose what we wanted to learn. You and I have been through this process of having a dominant conscious thought and remaining focused on it literally thousands of times throughout our lifetime. As such, we have developed a vast mental library of plans. We have a plan for walking, talking, reading, writing, driving a car, riding a bicycle, and on and on. We have a mental plan for everything that we do on a routine basis. When we go into these day-to-day activities, our subconscious pulls out the past plan and just executes on it. This process just happens automatically without us even being consciously aware of it.

Stop and think about it a second: How much conscious thought do you give to walking anymore? Right, none. You just think about where you want to go and begin to move in that direction. This is because you've already developed the plan to walk, so your subconscious mind can leverage your past plan. When you were a toddler, it didn't work this way because you hadn't yet developed the plan for walking.

Daniel Kahneman (remember, we met him before: he is the Nobel Prize–winning psychologist) taught me that as adults almost 95% of our life will be lived based on the subconscious plans we have developed in our past. Our brain will automatically look to see if we have a past plan we can leverage; even if a current situation doesn't perfectly match our past plan, our mind will default to following the existing plan. This is why each of us has habit patterns we follow in life. We get dressed the same way, brush our teeth the same way, and chew our food the same way. When we stop and look for them, we will see these patterns all over our life.

Ask yourself, do you tend to drive the same routes? Surf the same websites? Associate with the same people? Do you have a habit pattern to how your days tend to flow, the foods you like to eat, the television shows you like to watch, or the types of books you like to read?

More than 2,000 years ago, the Greek philosopher Aristotle spoke extensively about the significance of these mental habit patterns in his *Metaphysics Book V*, where he said,

"Mental habits are powerful factors in our lives. They are consistent, unconscious patterns that constantly, daily, express our character and produce our effectiveness or ineffectiveness."

As human beings, so much of our life will be defined by our past mental plans and the habit patterns they create for us. However, as Aristotle rightly pointed out, not all of our mental patterns are leading us in the right direction.

BREAKING THE PATTERN

When Daniel Kahneman helped me to understand the autopilot nature of our mind it was an eye-opener. I had never considered how these default mental programs guide us as we move through our days, or how they automatically define how we will act and react as common situations present themselves. Amazingly, we all have these mental habit patterns and yet, we don't even realize it.

Ask yourself: have you ever driven somewhere you have been many times before and when you got there, you didn't even remember driving there? Sure, we've all done that.

It is just one of those automatic mental patterns we follow. Just like we do for walking and talking.

These patterns all relate back to things that we learned in the past. However, although we typically think of learning as a positive thing, it isn't always. Many times, our destructive or negative mental patterns will tie back to traumas, fears, psychological injuries, or false beliefs.

Until my reboot, I never realized this. Nor was I able to see how so many of my actions related back to these negatively rooted subconscious habit patterns. Eating too much, drinking too much, spending too much—all of these were coping mechanisms, mental patterns that tied back to the trauma of my past.

What are your painkillers? What behaviors do you use to make you feel better? How do you distract yourself from the things that bother you? When you feel bad, what do you do to soothe yourself?

Take a moment and reflect: What are your patterns? What are the things that you repeatedly do? What are the ramifications of these reward systems, these default subconscious patterns you follow? Are they positive or negative? Do your patterns move you in the direction you want your life to go? Or are your patterns keeping you stuck in a rut, holding you back from the person you want to be?

These may seem like pretty simple questions. Remember, though, our patterns are automatic behaviors driven by our subconscious mind. In most cases, we won't even be consciously aware of them. So, our first step to breaking a negative mental pattern is to become aware that it exists. How do we do that?

First, you have to break out of autopilot mode. We are so accustomed to following our mental patterns that we just default into them. Amazingly, I found that many of the best aspects of our life is what we miss when we are in our autopilot mode, preoccupied with things that are far less important. I discovered the easiest way to recognize the pattern is just to train ourselves to slow down and recognize more of the everyday things in our day-to-day life.

For me, I started to do this when I was driving. I just made a game of it. I would set a goal to notice five unique things as I was driving somewhere. It forced me to turn off my autopilot and pay attention. I then expanded this to other areas of my life. I would work on noticing unique things as I was walking, working out, traveling, and so on. What I found is just this simple act of becoming more of a conscious observer began to turn off my mental autopilot mode.

Next, I began to pay more attention to my actions, the order in which I would do things, how I would spend my free time. I paid particular attention

(continued)

to actions that I knew weren't productive or leading me in the direction I wanted to go. When would I eat or drink too much? When did I have a craving for candy or the urge to buy something? This helped me to begin to see my behavioral patterns.

Then a funny thing began to happen. As I paid more attention to the patterns in my outer world, I began to notice more things in my inner world. Suddenly, I would notice an emotion as it began to arise. I would catch a negative thought as it crossed my mind. I began to see mental storms brewing before they erupted into anger. For the first time, I could see the patterns in my inner world.

Perhaps the most powerful thing to realize is that we don't have to be a victim to our thought patterns. We can notice them and then decide how we want to respond; do we want to accept them, ignore them, or even influence them in a way that drives positive change? We will talk more about this later in our conversation (Hint: this insight is a critical component of finding peace of mind.)

Changing Our Mind

Although most people's thoughts ebb and flow like the wind in the background, it is our ability to influence our thoughts that has the power to unshackle us. We can shift and change patterns of negative thoughts, override limiting thoughts, and let go of long-held oppressive thoughts.

However, this change will not happen without effort and consistent focus. More than 150 years ago, the poet Henry David Thoreau said,

> **As single footstep will not make a path**
> **on the earth,**
> **so, a single thought will not make a**
> **pathway in the mind.**
> **To make a deep physical path,**
> **we walk again and again.**
> **To make a deep mental path,**
> **we must think over and over the kind**
> **of thoughts**
> **we wish to dominate our lives.**

As Thoreau so eloquently pointed out, singular thoughts have very little power; repetitive thoughts become dominant and thus have great power. Why is this true? Remember, our dominant thoughts shape our beliefs.

So, how do we create new and better dominant thoughts? In an article published in the *Journal for Social Cognitive and Affective Neuroscience*, a joint team of researchers from the University of Pennsylvania, the University of Michigan, and the University of California found that using a tool called *affirmations* to redirect our thoughts has the power to not only rewire our brain but also change the physical structure of it.

Affirmations—defined:

Any statement or phrase that we consciously repeat to ourselves; a repetitive thought or assertation.

Consider this for a moment, research has shown that each of us has about 60,000 thoughts each day. However, each of these thoughts is not entirely new and unique. In fact, about 80% of our thoughts are actually repetitive thoughts. So, follow the logic: if any repetitive thought is an affirmation and 80% of our thoughts are repetitive, are you using affirmations already?

Without question. We all have thoughts—affirmations—that we repeat to ourselves. But here's the kicker: are all affirmations necessarily positive ones?

Be honest. Right, *no* they're not.

"I'm just not a morning person." "I can't function without a cup of coffee." "I'm no good at (math, sports, remembering people's names, and so on)." "I'll never be ..." "Things just don't seem to work out for me." "I'm so clumsy." "I'm always exhausted." "I just can't seem to (lose weight, get in shape, stop overeating, get a good job, save money, and so on)." "I don't think I'll ever be able to ..." "I'm not (smart enough, good enough, strong enough, talented enough, and so on)."

These are but a few of the laundry list of common negative affirmations. Sadly, most people inadvertently use affirmations to reinforce exactly what they don't want in their life.

We've all heard the old saying that someone is "lost in thought." What I realized through my reboot is that being lost in thought isn't just about a momentary lapse in concentration. No, it is far worse than that. People's entire lives get "lost in thought." Being lost in negative thoughts is something that consumes many people throughout their entire lifetime. It causes them to miss the best aspects of life, all while they are drowning in their negative affirmations.

Most people simply don't realize that they have a choice about what they think. They don't understand that they can influence their dominant thoughts in a positive direction.

What about you?

Here is perhaps the one of the most important questions you will ever be asked in your life:

Are you thinking right?

Are you thinking about who you really want to be in life? Are you thinking about where you want to be in life? Are you thinking about what you would really like to learn? Are you thinking about the positive aspects of your life, the things you are grateful for? Are you thinking about these things consistently every day? Have you made these into dominant thoughts that your subconscious mind can lock onto and manifest into your reality?

or

Are you thinking about what makes you mad? Are you thinking about the person who has hurt you? Are you thinking about what you don't want to do? Are you thinking about all that you lack? Are you thinking about what you don't like about yourself? Are you thinking about what scares you? Are these the thoughts that linger in your mind? Have you inadvertently allowed the negative thoughts to become dominant?

Remember,

"What you think, you become."

This is true regardless of whether you are thinking positive thoughts or negative thoughts.

WHAT ARE WE LOCKING ONTO?

In the latter part of the 1980s, a company I was working for had sponsored a young, up-and-coming public speaker to share some wisdom with us about how to be more successful in life.

When I first saw him, I couldn't help but notice that he was a rather large man with a big head and, seemingly, even bigger teeth. Yet he was dynamic and engaging and I soon found myself getting swept away by his enthusiasm.

Later, a few of us had the opportunity to go to an after-event reception and meet this gentleman. When I had a moment, I approached him and asked him if there were any good books that he could recommend. Without hesitation, Tony Robbins said, *Think and Grow Rich* by Napoleon Hill. (Little did I know at the time, two years later that giant of a man would host an infomercial that would launch him to international fame.)

I did a little research on the book he recommended and found out it had quite an interesting story behind it. In the early part of the 1900s, at the behest of industrialist Andrew Carnegie, a young newspaper reporter by the name of Napoleon Hill spent the better part of 20 years traveling across North America interviewing all of the most prominent and successful people of the era. He interviewed entrepreneurs and founders such as Henry Ford, King Gillette (founder of the shaving company Gillette), J. Ogden Armour (founder of Armour foods), Dr. David Starr Jordan (founding president of Stanford University), Elbert Gary (founder of U.S. Steel), and William Wrigley (founder of the Wrigley candy company). He interviewed inventors such as Thomas Edison (inventor of the light bulb and thousands of other things), Alexander Graham Bell (inventor of the telephone), and Wilbur Wright (coinventor of the airplane). He also interviewed US presidents, senators, and the leading thinkers of his day.

He took all that he learned from these prominent and successful people and used it in writing one of the most powerful self-help books ever published, *Think and Grow Rich*.

In this book, Napoleon Hill made a very powerful observation about the human mind when he said,

"The subconscious mind makes no distinction between constructive (positive) or destructive (negative) thought impulses. It works with the material we feed it. The subconscious mind will translate into reality a thought driven by fear just as readily as it will translate into reality a thought driven by courage or faith."

(*continued*)

What amazed me most about Hill's quote is the fact that our subconscious mind doesn't determine the worthiness of our dominant thoughts. Positive or negative, our subconscious locks onto and develops a plan to manifest into our reality whatever our dominant thoughts are.

In 1925, Henry Ford went to a group of his best engineers. He wanted them to design an inexpensive, reliable V8 engine from a single casting. After years of trial and error, all of his best and brightest engineers concluded that what Henry was asking them to do was physically impossible.

They went to Ford, showed him failed attempt after failed attempt, explaining the hundreds of different designs they tried. Ford refused to accept their excuses and told them to keep at it. Time and time again, they returned to Ford's office and tried to explain that what he was asking could not be done. Still, he refused to accept what they were telling him; keep at it he said.

Finally, after seven years of trying, his engineers found a solution and Ford's inexpensive, reliable, single-casting V8 engine became a reality. It transformed his company and gave the Ford Motor Company a significant advantage over every competitor.

When asked by a reporter why he kept pushing his engineers when they insisted his request was impossible, Henry Ford looked at the young reporter and said,

"If you think you can or you think you can't, you're right. I knew they could do it."

Although it took close to a century of additional research and a much deeper understanding of how our brain works, modern-day cognitive science has conclusively proven the wisdom of Henry Ford's quote. Whatever we ardently believe and refuse to give up on, our mind will eventually figure out how to achieve.

What Are Your Thoughts?

Stop and ask yourself, "What have I been thinking about myself?" Is it positive? Is it really who you want to be? If not, stop thinking these things. When these negative thoughts creep in (and they will, they do for everyone), consciously force them out with positive thoughts of who you want to be today and tomorrow.

Most people don't ever really recognize it, but you and I can consciously choose to think whatever we want to think. We don't have to just blindly accept the background thoughts that randomly roll through our head. We can choose our thoughts; I'll prove it to you.

I want you to think about an elephant right now. Picture what an elephant looks like. Got it? Good. Now, I want you to think about what a dog looks like. Picture a dog. Got it? Good. Now imagine that that dog is barking like crazy, maybe it sees an intruder coming into the house, or something like that. Last, I want you to think about a yellow house with a beautiful lush green lawn and a white fence in front of it. Can you picture that? Good.

Did your eyes actually see any of those things? Did an elephant just walk in front of you? Did a barking dog just run by? Did a yellow house magically appear out of nowhere? Nope, you generated all of those things as thoughts in your head. You influenced your thoughts. You just consciously chose to think about something.

If you can consciously choose to think about an elephant, why can't you consciously choose to think something positive instead of just accepting the random negative thought? If left to its own devices, our mind will automatically conjure up the negative thoughts, which is a sad vestige of our evolutionary programming. However, it is one we can and must consciously work to override.

Recognize you will make mistakes, you will screw things up, you will have bad days. You may say something, do something, or have something not work out the way you want. This happens to all of us. (It happened to me two days ago. I woke up the next day feeling tired, depressed, and worn out. Yes, I wanted to just stay in bed and feel sorry for myself. Yet, I recognized it was just one day, a bad day. I had the power to make sure one bad day didn't become a second bad day. I knew I could start again, with a better insight. These bad days make us stronger, not weaker—as long as we learn from them and then consciously give ourselves permission to let go of them.)

Don't get lost in the negative momentum and negative thoughts of who you were yesterday. That doesn't matter. What matters is who you want to be today and who you want to become tomorrow. Remember: everything is cumulative, so one bad day doesn't rob you of all the positive you have built, it just slows you down a step or two—big deal—it doesn't stop you dead in your tracks.

Remember, in life you don't get what you deserve, you get what you think about most often. Positive or negative, our thoughts define our beliefs. Our beliefs influence our actions, and our actions dictate our outcomes. It's cause and effect.

So, steer your life with conscious purpose. Focus your thoughts on what you want instead of what you don't want. Think over and over the kinds of thoughts you wish to dominate your life.

In the chapters ahead, I'll provide you with some affirmations, some optimal dominant thoughts I've collected from people I've interviewed and spent time with. These are the affirmations of world-class athletes, highly successful business executives, people who have scaled the highest mountains, conquered the greatest challenges, and overcome life's biggest obstacles. These affirmations have served these people well, and they will serve you equally well.

So, I'll give you the first two affirmations of your newly rebooted brain. Repeat them often in your mind.

- *I am ultimately responsible for what I choose to pay attention to and for the actions I choose to take.*
- *I have the limitless ability to learn.*

Keep reminding yourself that you get to choose what you think, that you can and must influence your thought process in the direction you want your life to move. Repeat these affirmations frequently to yourself. Make them into dominant thoughts that resonate in your mind. Your dominant thoughts will shape your beliefs and your beliefs will define your life.

You have within you far more power than you likely give yourself credit for. You have the power to script your life to guide it in the direction you most want. You have within you everything you need to succeed. It all starts with thinking differently.

There is a master list of all the affirmations you will want to use in your reboot at the end of the book.

PEOPLE–LEADER PERSPECTIVE

The simple phrases that we repeat as leaders become the affirmations of our people. This is one of the most important leadership tools that we can use to help our people to let go of limiting thoughts and embrace more empowering thoughts. It is how we, as leaders, can begin to move the motivational intelligence of our team in a more positive direction.

Rebooting Your Happiness and Letting Go of Limiting Perceptions

PEOPLE–LEADER PERSPECTIVE

Each of the chapters in Part 3 represents wonderful discussion starters to share with your team. I would encourage you to use each of them as individual prereads before a team meeting and then guide a discussion about the team's thoughts, impressions, and examples of where they have seen the topic of the chapter in effect.

These discussions will become a powerful way for you to dispel the myths that are holding your team back. They will also help you to develop higher levels of motivational intelligence across your team by reinforcing the right beliefs about *ultimate responsibility* and the *limitless ability to learn*.

CHAPTER 10

To Find Happiness, You Must "Unbecome"

We've spent the early part of our time together coming to understand ourselves, our real selves, the true person we were born to be. Then, we began to look at what goes wrong, where things get sideways and why. Last but not least, we began to put things back in the right place, to realign our mental operating system on the correct core beliefs, the optimal beliefs we were born with.

It is impossible to boot or reboot our brain if the fundamental programs of our mental operating system (*ultimate responsibility, limitless ability to learn*) are not properly in place. We've all experienced that moment of abject horror when our computer, tablet, or phone gives us the "screen of death" and refuses to start up. We fear all will be lost and our device won't work for us anymore. Although no one relishes having a broken piece of technology in their hand, what many people fail to realize is that the most important piece of technology they hold—their mind—has been broken, or at the very least compromised, for the better part of their life.

However, this isn't you. You know better, you are more aware, you now understand what the vast majority of people never will. You've begun to put things in place, the right place, where they always should have been. You now hold in in the palm of your hand the specialized knowledge and the insights of the world's greatest thinkers, Nobel Prize winners, and top neuroscientists. This, my friend, is a fundamental secret weapon for you in life. It is a differential advantage that will enable you to forever live in a space where most people can only dream of being.

Now it is time for us to build on your rebooted mental operating system. Our next process will help you shift the critical perspectives that confine so many. Through this discussion, you will see how letting go of the myths and embracing the truths will enable you to find lasting happiness and, ultimately, the peace of mind that we long for. I'm looking forward to this next part of our journey together. Let's get started . . .

HAPPINESS ISN'T A DESTINATION, IT'S A MINDSET

Years ago, Michelle started to practice yoga. She has often talked about what a transformative impact it has had on her life and her mindset. One word that has frequently come up is *gratitude*. As I was thinking about the topic of happiness this seemed like a good place to start.

Diving into the topic, I discovered the work of Robert Emmons. He is a psychologist and professor at University of California, Davis, who has spent the better part of two decades studying the benefits and impact of gratitude on one's happiness.

Through his research he has found that gratitude can significantly increase both our psychological happiness and physical well-being. I was curious why. Here is how Robert explains it:

First, gratitude is an affirmation of goodness. We affirm that there are good things in the world and benefits we've received. This doesn't mean that life is perfect; it doesn't ignore complaints, burdens, and hassles. But when we look at life as a whole, gratitude encourages us to identify some amount of goodness in our life.

The second part of gratitude is figuring out where that goodness comes from. We recognize the sources of this goodness as being outside of ourselves. It didn't stem from anything we necessarily did ourselves in which we might take pride. We can appreciate positive traits in ourselves, but I think true gratitude involves a humble dependence on others: We acknowledge that other people—or even higher powers, if you're of a spiritual mindset—gave us many gifts, big and small, to help us achieve the goodness in our lives.

As I listened to Robert, I could certainly see how shifting more of the focus of our thoughts to what we are appreciative of or grateful for would improve our perspective and positively affect our happiness. In essence, we are reconditioning our evolutionarily negative brain to recognize the good that is all around us every day.

With the clutter of my negative thoughts and limiting beliefs cleaned up after my reboot, I was able to see, appreciate, and acknowledge more the positive aspects of life. I felt more grateful for everything, from the air that I was now able to once again breathe to the time I got to spend with people. I could understand the impact gratitude had on our happiness, yet it still it felt like there was another piece missing, some component of happiness that was critical for a reboot.

Right around this time, a friend introduced me to Mo Gawdat. Mo is an Egyptian-born software engineer and former Google senior executive. Sadly, in 2014, Mo lost his 21-year-old son, Ali, to a tragic medical error. For any of us as parents, it is hard to imagine the pain and sorrow of losing a child.

As Mo and his wife were trying to cope with their loss, he realized his son wouldn't want his legacy to be leaving his parents to live a life of grief and sorrow. So, Mo decided he was going to once again try to find happiness. Using a software engineer's logical approach, he set off on a quest to deconstruct what makes us find happiness and made a rather startling discovery in the process. *The secret to happiness is often found in less, not more.*

Although that statement may seem a little confusing on the surface, allow me a moment to explain. I was always of the thought process that happiness was something that was going to be found hand-in-hand with abundance. In other words, once I got enough (love, health, possessions, money, and so on), I would finally be happy. In my mind, having more was what was going to make me happy. I believed happiness came as a result of more external things. So, this is what I chased.

It was Mo who taught me that my approach to happiness would never allow me to find it. What he discovered as he was trying to find happiness after his son's death was that happiness can be found only when two conditions are met.

First Condition for Happiness: When the Realities of Our Life Exceed Our Expectations

When I stepped back and reflected on it, this was the pathway I was following. I was trying to make my realities, the outcomes of my life, bigger and better. In hindsight, I now realize that the problem with my strategy was my expectations were constantly readjusting as my realities grew. As I became more successful, my expectations for my life just kept getting bigger. It was a never-ending arms race with no pathway to winning.

(continued)

Imagine being out of shape and walking on a treadmill. Slowly, over time, your conditioning becomes stronger and you get more fit. However, as this happens, the treadmill starts moving faster. The more fit you get, the faster the treadmill goes. It is always running just a little bit faster than you are fit, and you always feel like you can never keep up.

This was the reality of my life. I seemingly had a lot, yet it just never seemed good enough, complete enough. It never quite felt whole. I just could never seem to outrun, outearn, or outlive my expectations.

I think this is the pathway many people walk each day. It is a pathway that can only lead to unhappiness. Why? Because advertisers, marketing companies, manufacturers, and social media companies all profit from telling us how our life should be, what it should look like, what we need to be happy. They are the treadmill that keeps speeding up our perspective on, or expectation of what our life should be. Their goal is to fuel our constant sprint for more.

Second Condition for Happiness: When We Have Removed the Things That Make Us Unhappy

Think about that for a moment. You could be wearing the most comfortable pair of $3,000 custom shoes. These shoes may have been painstakingly handcrafted over a period of months to perfectly fit your feet; yet, if you had a pebble in your sock, they wouldn't feel right. You wouldn't find the exquisite comfort of those shoes until you removed the pebble.

This same analogy applies to the broader aspects of our life: more stuff layered on top of things that are making us fundamentally unhappy will never fix things. They may serve as a temporary distraction; however, the underlying issues will always resurface, and unhappiness will follow.

I had never really considered this perspective. So, it was this realization that led me on a quest to discover **what makes us fundamentally unhappy?**

Before You Can Have, You Must "Unbecome"

Years ago, my mentor shared a simple phrase that has always stuck with me. He said,

"Before you can have in life, you must first become."

As I reflected on that statement it inherently made sense to me. I mean, before Michelle could work in the labor room delivering babies, she had to learn about the human body and how it works; she had to become a nurse. Before someone can electrically wire up houses, install circuit breakers and outlets, they have to become an electrician. Before someone can become a great husband, wife, or partner, they must become a good listener and communicator. The list goes on and on.

However, as I sit here today reflecting on my life before my reboot, I realize that despite understanding this fundamental truth, in my past, I could easily point to countless times where my own limiting mindset caused me to resist the process of becoming.

In fact, when I got quiet, still, and looked back, I realized that in many, many areas of my life, I had never really given myself permission to become good at anything. I was okay in some areas, maybe better in others, and frankly, there were some areas where I was pretty dismal.

It wasn't that I didn't know what to do to make me happier or more successful. Most of us know that we should eat better, exercise more, save more money, spend less, and become better versions of ourselves. These are not some closely held secrets to a life better lived. Yet for some reason, even though we know what we should and shouldn't be doing, we oftentimes do things that are counterproductive to the person we really want to be, and this just further perpetuates our own unhappiness.

Why is this?

That was the question that I posed to Shawn Achor, a professor of positive psychology at Harvard. He explained to me that research is showing that it's not necessarily our reality that shapes our happiness but rather the perspective through which our brain views the world. He said, "If I know everything about your external world, I can only predict about 10% of your long-term happiness. Ninety percent of your long-term happiness is predicted not by the things that are happening in your outside world but by the perspective with which your brain looks at the world."

Shawn's response made me begin to think about the limiting perspectives that I may have locked onto. Perspectives that caused me to view myself, other people, and the world at large from a constrained viewpoint. Perspectives that held me back, restricting my actions and confining both my outcomes and happiness.

We may not realize it, but we all have limiting perspectives. They have been conditioned into us. Not necessarily by evildoers, people with bad intent, or some villainous mastermind cult of elites; no, limiting perspectives are oftentimes like a baton that gets handed from parent to child, reinforced by societal conditioning and anchored through common phrases that are often repeated and thus easily come to mind.

So, ask yourself, do you want to be happier? Do you want to become more? Do you want to enjoy more? Do you want to experience more?

I know I do. And likely so do you?

So, if we want more, we first have to become more. However, before we can become, we must let go of the limiting perspectives that are holding us back.

Simply put, we have to "unbecome" before we can rebecome. We must remove those pebbles in our shoes that are causing us discomfort and misshaping our perspective.

What I realized through my reboot was a major portion of my positive experience happened as a direct result of letting go of the long-held limiting perspectives that clouded my judgment, misinformed my thoughts, and in many ways, made me do stupid things that held me back from the life I most wanted.

My reboot helped me to unbecome. This is the next step in our journey together.

Clearing the Clutter in Your Mental Operating System

In many regards, my life path has been somewhat nontraditional. However, I am fortunate to be a part of an organization that has allowed me to spend the last 30 years traveling the world consulting with major corporations, interacting with thought leaders, and helping people to succeed. Throughout this journey, I have spoken with thousands of groups and from each, people have shared their experiences, insights, and wisdom. Over the years, I have done my best to collect their stories, to learn from their struggles and from their triumphs. I never knew the day would come when all of this wisdom would serve an even higher purpose. However, here we sit together today, and I want to share the insights gained through more than 2 million miles in airplanes, interacting with people from six continents and in 95+ countries.

On great reflection (and a near-death experience and mental reboot), what all of these conversations have taught me is that there are eight myths, misperceptions that distort our reality and cloud the world as we see it. These myths cause people to possess a wrongfully skewed view of themselves and how the world works. They create false expectations and flawed perspectives that cause people to act and react in limiting ways. These are the pebbles that create our unhappiness.

The Truths and Myths

You see, there are a handful of simple truths that give us the power to shape our world, define our path, and achieve those things that we most desire in life. If you and I accept these truths, we will destine ourselves to a life of happiness and fulfillment.

Conversely, if we deny these truths and buy into the misshappen perspectives, the myths that shackle so many, we will destine ourselves to become a victim: a victim of circumstance, a victim of our environment, a victim of all the things we have absolutely no control over in life. Remember, victims never win and rarely are they ever happy.

In the chapters ahead, we will explore the subtle and insidious ways that society conditions our mindset and shapes our perspectives. It sells us the myths every day through simple, oft-repeated phrases and comments from others. I didn't realize it but prior to my reboot, I was a card-carrying member of the mediocrity club. I had bought into many of the limiting perspectives that hold people back and trap them in a whirlwind of unhappiness and disillusionment. It's a world where so much seems out of reach and much seems beyond our control, it's a world where peace of mind is little more than a wishful pipe dream.

However, my reboot taught me that we can rip up our mediocrity membership card and reshape the way we look at ourselves and the world. You see, our perspective is fully our choice. You don't have to accept the limiting perspective of those around you. You don't have to hold onto the debilitating perspectives that were thrust on you by your parents, teachers, coaches, past girlfriends or boyfriends, and so on. Recognize that for many of these people it was their own limiting perspectives that they were passing on. They themselves had broken aspects of their brain, so this is what they handed to you. As the old saying goes, "Misery loves company . . . (and so, too, does mediocrity)."

Perhaps at some point, they too will want to follow in your footsteps and reboot their thought process. However, for now let's just focus on you.

So, choose wisely because few things will shape your happiness and satisfaction more than the perspectives you hold onto.

Are you ready to get started on the next phase of your reboot? Are you ready to begin building the better version of you? Are you ready to unbecome? Good! Let's get started in the next chapter.

CHAPTER 11

Myth: Some People Have "It," but You Don't

What is it that enables someone to become good at something? Is it some innate ability? Some unique skill set that they were gifted with? Is the ability to become good at something bestowed on some but not others? Is the ability to excel woven into the DNA of only a select few?

When you look at those people who have become really good at something, it seems like they have a relative ease at which they are able to execute on a given skill.

Just listen to billionaire Warren Buffett dole out investment advice. Watch a video of rock star Eric Clapton as he rips through a blues guitar lick. See gold medal–winning gymnast Simone Biles do a no-handed backflip. Watch basketball great Michael Jordan as he soars through the air to dunk a basketball. Listen to Nobel Prize–winning biochemist Jennifer Doudna explain the process for editing genes.

When we look at the iconic people in any field, it seems like the gap is so big between what they can do and what you and I are capable of, it is easy to convince ourselves that they must have some innate ability, some naturally granted level of talent that we simply don't possess.

Certainly, when looking at the capabilities of billionaires, sports stars, world-class musicians, or top scientists the gap between us and them is pretty dramatic. So, it's easy to say that they have "it" but we don't.

However, what most people fail to recognize is that they make this same comparison on a smaller scale every day. Just look around. You will see example after example.

So often people will look at the great mother or father across the street as they're playing with their kids in the front yard and think to themselves, "That person is just a natural at parenting." Or as they struggle to get in shape or lose weight, they look at their physically fit friend and think, "It just comes easy to them."

Frankly, almost any time someone struggles at something, it is pretty common for them to look at others who are really good in that area of life and think to themselves, "That person is just a natural, it just comes easier to them." After all, that must be the reason why *they* are able to excel, why *they* can succeed, and I can't—right?

Well, what if it's not? What if the idea that it just comes easier for other people is patently false. What if nobody was born with any innate talent. What if everybody else had to work just as hard as you do to learn something, to improve, and to achieve some level of success. What if the idea of natural talent is just an excuse we use (yup, I've used it, too) to justify our fears, our self-doubts, and our insecurities.

What if we've been wrong all these years?

Exploring the Idea of Talent

In his famous Nike commercial from 2008, six-time NBA Champion Michael Jordan said:

Maybe it's my fault.

Maybe I led you to believe it was easy, when it wasn't. Maybe I made you think that my highlights started at the free throw line and not in the gym. Maybe I made you think that every shot I took was a game winner. Maybe it is my fault that I didn't let you see that failure gave me strength, that my pain was my motivation. Maybe I led you to believe that basketball was a God-given gift and not something I worked for every single day of my life.

Or maybe, you're just making excuses.

One of the most pervasive and destructive self-limiting beliefs is that of natural ability. This insidious perspective is a like cancer that eats away at our belief in our *ultimate responsibility* and *limitless ability to learn* because it destroys our confidence and willingness to practice. It limits what we give ourselves permission to go after and causes people to give up when things become challenging. The concept of natural-born ability becomes the perfect excuse for mediocrity.

THE ELEPHANT IN THE ROOM

What about child prodigies, world-class athletes, maestro composers, and virtuoso musicians? How can it possibly be said that these people don't have innate talents, God-gifted capabilities that we don't possess? That must be the reason they can excel and we can't, right? This was the question that resonated in my mind (and likely yours as well).

After all, wasn't Wolfgang Mozart a child prodigy who was writing symphonies at the age of nine—how can that possibly happen without natural abilities?

It was sociologist Malcolm Gladwell who helped me reconcile this in my mind. Gladwell spent years researching this idea of innate talent and natural ability. In fact, he wrote extensively about it in his bestseller, *Outliers: the Story of Success*.

The question of Mozart's early accomplishments also puzzled Gladwell, so he set about understanding the true backstory. The real story, not the hyperbole or legend that often gets handed down over time. Here is what he found out.

Wolfgang Mozart was born in 1719. His father was a composer, music teacher, and noted violinist, so young Mozart was exposed to music from the time he was an infant. His father frequently took Mozart on trips to meet the most acclaimed composers of his day. He also was a dedicated teacher who spent hours working with young Wolfgang, helping him to perfect both his ability to play various instruments and to write musical compositions.

So, with the help of his father, Mozart was in fact composing at a young age. However, when Gladwell went and looked at Mozart's early works, they were relatively simple and lacked the sophistication that his later works were noted for. Basically, Mozart's early compositions were about what you would expect from a nine-year-old kid who had been extensively schooled in musical composition by a dedicated parent. Mozart's best works wouldn't come

(continued)

until he was in his late 20s after he had thousands of hours of practice writing music.

Was Mozart really a child prodigy? Was he born a virtuoso? The evidence would point to the answer being *no*. He did become a highly accomplished composer through a lot of practice, though.

Okay, what about world-class athletes, Olympians, and gold medal winners; surely they must possess natural talent to excel within the world of sports, right?

Let's look at the best example we can find. US swimmer Michael Phelps is by a large margin the most successful Olympian of all time. He holds 28 Olympic medals, 23 of them being gold (the next closest Olympian is Russian gymnast Larisa Latynina, who holds 18).

If there was ever a "natural" athlete, Michael Phelps must surely be one. To succeed at this level, he must have had innate talents with regard to swimming. How else could he have been so dominant?

Well, let's look at the facts. Michael Phelps began to swim competitively at the age of seven. At 11 he began to work with coach Bob Bowman, perhaps the most well-regarded swimming coach of all time. Bowman is also known for his "drill sergeant–like" coaching style and the relentless ways that he pushes his athletes.

A young Michael Phelps spent six days a week working in the pool. On average swimming about 50 miles every week, which is more than 8 miles a day, six days a week, every week. (By comparison, the average person only walks about 2 miles a day. Can you imagine swimming a distance that is 4× greater than you walked yesterday?)

So, certainly, Phelps had prodigious practice when it came to swimming. However, he also had one other significant benefit—genetic advantage.

Wait, didn't I just say there is no such thing as innate ability? Follow me: this is where a lot of people get confused. Innate talent and natural ability imply some given level of skill, something that is predisposed. Genetic advantage implies no given level of skill or innate aptitude, just a body type that lends itself to a given sport. See the difference? It's an important one that a lot of people miss.

So, let's look at Michael Phelps as an example here. If you are a swimmer, having long arms gives you more leverage to pull your body through the water, having relatively shorter legs creates less drag, big hands and big feet provide a certain "duck-like" advantage to create greater speed. Michael Phelps has all of these. You could say he has a near perfect body for a competitive swimmer. Did this give him an edge? Without question.

However, without the years of dedication, long hours of practice, and intense conditioning, Phelps would never have become a world-class swimmer. When asked if he was a natural-born swimming champion, Michael Phelps himself said,

"Saying I was born to win is an absolutely absurd claim."

Think about it. Likely we all know someone who has big hands and big feet, yet they would struggle to swim one length of a pool, let alone eight miles in a day. Genetic advantage is great to have, but without consistent practice and hard work, it's pretty much worthless.

In an exhaustive study, cognitive scientists at Tufts University and the University of Melbourne researched hundreds of supposed "child prodigies" and "world-class performers" and found no evidence of natural ability or innate talent. The bottom line: they found that no one is great without work.

So where does this leave you and me? Well, first, let's be painfully honest with ourselves. In all likelihood, our opportunity to go to the Olympics or win a world championship in sports—well, that ship has sailed, my friend. So, we may need to let that dream go. I hate to be the bearer of bad news, but sometimes we all need a little reality check.

So, at this stage of our lives, genetic advantage isn't going to mean much. Very likely, for you and me moving forward, having big hands or big feet isn't going to matter much. Having a willingness to consistently practice and leveraging the right mindset as we do—that is all that is going to matter.

Accepting Reality

Similar to many people, prior to my reboot, I could see my shortcomings with incredible clarity, but I looked at my potential to learn through a fog-like haze.

Nearly everywhere I looked I was immersed in this concept of natural ability. I heard the term over and over as I watched sporting events on TV, listened to great musicians play, or read about the exploits of some supposed child prodigy. I just blindly accepted that things were easier for other people than they were for me. This was my reality; it was my truth, although it wasn't really true at all.

The truth is, nobody starts out great at something from day one. People become good (at anything) by first making a conscious choice about what they want to be good at. Then they must consistently practice, reflect, and refine. It is only through time and hard work that people improve. It is more about effort and time than innate talent and ability.

We just aren't being fair to ourselves expecting that we will be instantly successful at anything. If things are hard at first, that is how they are supposed to be. It just doesn't pay to get discouraged and give up on ourselves when something is tough to learn.

International chess grandmaster Josh Waitzkin once said,

"The moment that we believe that success is predetermined by an engrained level of ability, we will be brittle in the face of adversity."

Looking back at everything you are good at, isn't it true that you have become better over time, with practice? Just think about this statement for a moment:

Every strength you have today was once a weakness of yours.

Stop and consider this simple fact. You used to suck at every single thing you're good at, every single thing you do each day, everything you do today with a level of effortless excellence:

- Walking
- Talking
- Tying your shoes
- Driving a car
- Getting dressed
- Reading
- Writing

I could go on and on. The list of things you and I do each day is incredibly long.

Think about it: every one of these things, we used to suck at. Yup, that's right: they were all awkward, uncomfortable, clumsy things when we first started out. Yet with time, practice, and refinement, we now are good at all of these things; we do them every day and don't even give them any thought at all.

Earlier, we talked about learning to walk. How did that work out the first time you stood up? (Well, you likely don't remember, so let me remind you.) Yup, you sucked at it. But how much time, energy, and thought do you put into walking now? Not much. You turned that weakness into a strength.

Remember learning to tie your shoes? That was a tricky one. All those crossing of laces and loops. It seemed overwhelming, confusing, and nearly impossible when we first watched someone else do it. We sucked at that one, too, at first. Now, you and I can tie our shoes without even looking. That's another weakness we turned into a strength.

Shall I go on, or do you get the point?

Throughout the course of our life, you and I have turned thousands of weaknesses into strengths. In fact, you're really good at turning weaknesses into strengths; you've done it again and again.

Yet why is it that for the common things, like walking and talking, we readily accept that we all have the ability to learn these things? However, for other things, perhaps those less common, like playing an instrument, painting, or playing a sport, we readily accept that other people have innate talents and abilities that we don't. We believe that they can do it, but we can't. Why is this?

DON'T EXPECT ANYTHING WILL BE EASY AT FIRST

When I was 15 years old, my best friend Ned and I decided we wanted to learn to play the guitar. We went down to our local music store, took some of the money we had saved up from mowing lawns and delivering newspapers, and bought two acoustic guitars.

The store had a guy in his 30s who gave guitar lessons. Ned and I convinced him to teach us to play. He taught us some simple scales and chords and sent us off to practice them.

I struggled to make my notes sound right and couldn't get my fingers to move across the guitar frets with any ease or grace. My rhythm wasn't any better and I just couldn't seem to get the hang of strumming either. Candidly, nothing about playing the guitar came easily.

Pretty soon, I had convinced myself that although I loved the sound of the instrument, playing the guitar just wasn't for me. I thought that I just didn't

(continued)

have the ability or aptitude necessary to play. So, the guitar went into its case and was slid under my bed. It became one more item on the long list of failures in my life. Just another reminder of something I wanted to do but couldn't because I just wasn't good enough.

What made it even more painful was I just assumed it came easier to Ned. Rather than recognizing that he was practicing more than I was, I thought he was more of a "natural" musician and that's why he could make better sounds come out of the guitar. I was too ashamed and embarrassed to admit any of this to Ned, so I just told him I decided I didn't want to play anymore.

Then I blinked my eyes and 40 years went by.

After I got out of the hospital and my brain rebooted, I was still trying to rehab my body and recover from the physical effects of COVID. I also had taken time off from work to get my health back in order.

As I was reconnecting with friends, updating everyone on how I was doing and thanking them for all their well-wishes, I was chatting with Ned one afternoon and we got talking about the guitar.

He had stuck with it over the years, and because of thousands of hours of practice, Ned had become a pretty accomplished guitar player. So, I asked him if he would teach me to play, and a new journey has started for me. I'm now nine months into playing the guitar. Don't get me wrong, I still suck at it, but I suck at it less than I did nine months ago.

I don't really believe I am destined to become a guitar virtuoso. I do believe that I can become the best guitarist I will allow myself to be.

All that matters is that we give ourselves permission to make a choice and we are willing to keep practicing.

What If You Could Learn Anything?

Just imagine for a moment how differently our lives, yours and mine, would look if we a hadn't been conditioned to believe in the concept of natural ability. Think of the different choices we would have made.

The fear of failure, the fear of not being good enough, the fear of making a mistake would all cease to exist within our consciousness. Rather than being ruled by fears, self-doubts, and negativity, we would view life as a virtually limitless opportunity to learn, grow, and improve ourselves.

We would approach learning everything with an open mind. We would willingly practice however much was required to excel. The more we practiced, the better we would become. This would be true for anything we desired to learn.

If we wanted to get better at math, we could. If we wanted to learn to play an instrument, we could. If we wanted to be our best at playing a given sport, we could. If we desired to become proficient at a certain job, we could.

Without this limiting belief, we could become good (maybe even great) at whatever we set our mind to achieve. Imagine how limitless our life would be. Imagine what we could have accomplished and achieved in our past if we truly allowed ourselves to let go of the limiting belief that others could excel but we couldn't.

Well, we can't change our past. So, instead imagine what you can do in your future! The great statesman Nelson Mandela once said,

"Education is the most powerful weapon you can use to change the world."

Don't worry about comparing yourself to others. They may be ahead of you or behind you on the learning curve. Compare yourself to what you were capable of yesterday. Are you a little bit better today? Have you leveraged your practice? If you can answer yes to those questions, you are on the right path. Soon days of practice turn to months of practice, and you find yourself light-years ahead of where you started. Remember, permission and practice is where it all starts.

Changing Our Perspective: The Truth About Talent and Ability

When I set out on a quest to figure out the truth about this elusive topic—are some people just more innately gifted—one name kept coming to the top of the list of people to speak with: Swedish psychologist Dr. Anders Ericsson.

Ericsson had spent more than four decades studying the world's top ballet dancers, surgeons, musicians, athletes, and actors, all in an effort to prove or disprove the notion that talent is naturally or innately gifted. He conducted countless studies on high-level performers, wrote more than 300 papers, and authored five books based on what he learned. In essence, through his work, he became the world's foremost leading expert on what it takes to become an expert at something.

I couldn't think of anyone more qualified to ask; as such, I set out to find someone who could introduce me to him. Sadly, I soon discovered that he had passed away a few months earlier. So, I did the next best thing, I immersed myself in his work and began to study his studies. There was one in particular that really stood out.

With his team of researchers, Anders Ericsson went to the Berlin Academy of Music, a school world-renowned for producing international soloist-level violinists. Basically, a school that is recognized for training the best violinists in the world.

Without the students knowing, Ericsson asked the administrators of the school to split the class of violinists into three groups:

- Those who they felt would make it to the highest level, becoming an international soloist in a major philharmonic
- Those who were "merely good enough" to be first or second chair violin in internationally renowned symphony orchestras
- Those who would go on to become music teachers who would train younger violinists

Ericsson and his research team then collected data and conducted detailed interviews with the students, the student's teachers, and the student's parents. They also asked each student to keep a detailed log of the time they spent practicing each day. These interviews and the data collected resulted in a detailed profile about each of the students which he and his research team then analyzed.

What they found was that the violinists from each of the three groups had extremely similar background stories. They'd all started playing at about the same age. They all had decided to pursue music as a profession at about the same age. They all had similar instructional backgrounds.

In fact, there was only one statistic that clearly separated the groups and that was *practice hours*. Those violinists from the first two groups (the top-tier soloists and the first and second chair violinists) practiced on average 24.3 hours per week. The violinists who were destined to become teachers practiced on average 9.3 hours per week.

But surely the very best violinists, those who were destined to become the international soloists must have had some natural ability that made them stand out. Right?

Well, Ericsson's research team was also able to define the difference between these great violinists and the good violinists as well. That too came down to practice. The very best violinists had, on average, racked up 7,410 lifetime practice hours. Those destined to be ensemble players had only managed 5,301 lifetime practice hours.

That's a differential of 2,109 hours. That's right, the only difference between the great violinists and the good ones was the best violinists had practiced 30% more.

Imagine practicing something 3 hours a day, 6 days a week, 52 weeks of the year—it would take you over two years to make up those 2,109 hours.

Think of it this way—if you played chess against a friend who had played 2,100 hours more than you, would you expect them to be a better chess player than you are? Might that extra practice, those additional hours playing, make it look like it was easier for that person? All that additional practice may even make it appear like that person was a "natural" at playing.

Is it even fair for you or me to expect that we would be better than someone who had practiced something for more than 2,100 additional hours? Of course not.

Certainly, the extra 2,100 hours of practice would give them an edge. Why wouldn't you expect their skill level to be better than yours?

Now take the word *chess* out of the example and substitute any other activity—speaking a language, skiing, computer programming, playing basketball, writing, painting, taking pictures, playing the guitar, editing videos, cooking, investing, doing a certain job, anything you can think of. Do you think that someone with 2,100 more hours of practice would appear more "naturally talented" than you? Of course, they would!

In more than 300 studies of high performers, Anders Ericsson consistently found that the facts clearly showed that nobody is naturally gifted and nobody is great without practice. You and I were born with the "ability to become" good at whatever we choose to become good at. It all comes down to practice.

What Anders Ericsson found in his research is that, on average, it takes thousands of hours of deliberate practice to become our best at any given skill. Now what is deliberate practice? It is approaching an activity in a way that is explicitly designed to improve our performance, reaching for objectives just beyond our current level of competence, getting meaningful feedback on our results, and doing it all with a high level of repetition.

Vladimir Horowitz, a man considered to be one of the greatest pianists who has ever lived, once said,

"The difference between ordinary and extraordinary is practice."

Peel back the layers, look beyond the myths and hyperbole that make for great fodder in the media, and the truth becomes readily apparent. There is no DNA, no gene, that automatically makes someone a great chess player, a superstar athlete, a world-class musician, a top skier, or a great leader. What you practice most often is what you will get better at doing.

Now I want you to imagine what you could accomplish if you truly believed you could be good at anything you set your mind to. What could you achieve if you truly believed that you could not fail? If you would willingly practice a given skill set for thousands of hours, there would be nothing that would stand in the way. Believe in yourself. Believe in your *limitless ability to learn*. Believe in the fact that the efforts you put into today will make you better tomorrow.

Five Steps for Rebooting Our Improved Perspective

1. Pick something you would like to learn or get better at doing. Pick something new or pick a weakness you would like to turn into a strength.
2. Do you know someone who is better at this skill or ability than you are? Ask them to mentor you.
3. Where can you go to learn more about this skill or ability? (Google online courses, look for YouTube videos, check Amazon, your local bookstore, or library for resources where you can learn more, and so on.)

4. Set up a practice/learning schedule (be realistic; start with 10 minutes a day).
5. Create a challenge or goal to help you map your progress. Don't be overly aggressive; be realistic, such as where would you like to be in two weeks?

Thinking "Right" Activity

Remember, our dominant thoughts shape our beliefs, and our beliefs drive our actions. So, a major portion of our reboot hinges on letting go of limiting thoughts/perspectives and replacing them with new and better dominant thoughts that are rooted in the truth. Here are two affirmations that will help you make this important transition. Repeat them often in your mind.

- *The more I practice, the better I perform.*
- *Permission to try and persistence in practice are what my success is built on.*

There is a sequential plan of all of the actions you will want to follow for your reboot at the end of the book.

PEOPLE–LEADER PERSPECTIVE

The myth of natural ability and innate talent are two deadly doubts that erode a person's belief in their *limitless ability to learn.* Helping your people to stop comparing themselves to others and attaching feedback to their sense of self-worth is key here.

Everybody has the *limitless ability to learn.* Some will learn more quickly than others; however, this doesn't mean that the late bloomers can't improve. If someone's beliefs are in the right place, and they give themselves permission to practice and reflect, they have the key to learning, adjusting, and adapting to whatever life might put before them.

CHAPTER 12

Myth: Circumstances Control Your Destiny

How often have you heard that to succeed you have to be in the *right* place at the *right* time? Look at how easily that statement comes to mind. Over and over, we have heard the right place, right time myth.

Why is this myth so dangerous? It is dangerous because it conditions a person's perspective in a way that they believe that happiness and success are more about circumstance than substance. It is about having the good fortune to be in the right place when success comes knocking on the door. It is dangerous because it causes us to wait, hoping that situations will conspire to drive our success, rather than taking action today to build our success and create our happiness.

I once heard it said that we are all citizens of the same nation: the nation of *procrastination*. It's easy to put things off till tomorrow, next week, or even next year. It is easy to wait, dream, hope, and wish that the circumstances of tomorrow will be better, and success will appear on our doorstep. However, the right place, right time myth just falls flat on further scrutiny.

STOP WAITING FOR THE BEST THINGS IN LIFE TO HAPPEN TO YOU

I met Michelle in high school. She was 15 and I was 16. I was smitten from first sight. We dated all through high school and college. After we graduated, Michelle began pursuing her career in nursing, and I began mine in business. We were building our lives.

After about eight years together, my parents and friends began asking me, "Are you two ever going to get married?" I guess in my mind I always knew we would be together, but for some reason, I just kept waiting to ask her to marry me.

Then one day a coworker and early mentor of mine asked me, "What the hell is the holdup? Why haven't you asked Michelle to marry you yet?"

I sat and thought about it and replied, "I guess I'm just waiting for the perfect moment; you know, like when I walk out of the apartment and a beam of sunshine hits me, and I hear the angels singing, then I'll know it is the right time to ask."

He just looked at me like I was some kind of idiot (which I was) and said, "Dave, that only happens in the movies. Can you see yourself sitting on a porch with her when you're 75 years old and still having something to talk about?"

"Yeah, I can," I replied.

"Then she's the one; stop stalling," he said.

Two days later I bought an engagement ring and asked her if she would marry me. We've been married for 30 years now.

Many times, the best aspects of our life are just one decision away. We just need to change our perspective and stop waiting for the perfect time and place to appear. It is already there, right in front of us.

Changing Our Perspective: The Truth About Being in the Right Place at the Right Time

Just imagine being on the ground floor of a rapidly growing internet company. A company that was about to take the industry by storm. A company that was preparing for a public offering that was set to make the founders and early employees into multimillionaires or billionaires. Think what you could do with your newfound financial freedom. Think of the places you could travel to. Wouldn't it be great if you could just find yourself in *that* right place at *that* right time?

As one of the founders of Twitter, the $50+ billion-dollar social media company that taught us to convey our most profound thoughts in 140 characters, Noah Glass was certainly in the right place at the right time. Yet being in this right place and right time didn't make Noah a billionaire, or even a millionaire. *Why?* Well, he was kicked out of the company that he helped found because he hadn't yet become the type of leader that the early investors felt that they needed.

What about Sandy Lerner, who cofounded Cisco Systems, a multinational goliath in the communication, networking, and IT fields. A $180+ billion-dollar company that *Forbes* magazine ranks as one of the most valuable brands in the world.

Sandy was unceremoniously fired from the company she founded and never realized the tremendous abundance that was created as the company grew. *Why?* The team of people around her didn't feel she had the skills necessary to take the company to the next level. She hadn't become the person she needed to be to lead the organization.

Both of these people were undeniably in the right place at the right time. Yet success eluded them. *Why?*

Perhaps success requires something more than just being at the right place at the right time. What it requires is being the *right person* in the *right place* at the *right time.*

There are countless examples like Noah Glass and Sandy Lerner. People who were in the right place at the right time, but they were the *"wrong person."* As such, success marched right by them.

So how do you become the *right* person? The caliber of person who is truly capable of capitalizing on opportunity when it presents itself. Certainly, honing and refining the right skill sets plays an important part. After all, life rarely rewards the mediocre.

As such, one must ask themselves, what skills will be required for me to achieve success? To answer this question, look at others who have accomplished similar achievements. With this insight, you can better define what specific skills you will need to become better at.

However, far more important than developing the right skill sets is developing the right mindset. Throughout history there are countless stories of people who overcame seemingly insurmountable obstacles to achieve success. What is it that caused these people to persist where others gave up? Why were they able to stay focused and motivated despite all the setbacks? Why did they so steadfastly believe that it was possible when everyone around them was telling them it wasn't going to work out?

It was these people's mindset that caused them to beat the odds. They weren't afraid to "think" differently.

Social entrepreneur and Nobel Prize–winner Muhammad Yunus once said,

"Mindsets play strange tricks on us. We see things the way our minds have instructed our eyes to see."

23,000 PEOPLE CAN'T ALL BE WRONG

Harvard psychologist David McClelland spent the better part of his career looking for what differentiates people. He was a pioneer in understanding human motivation and the underpinnings of what drove achievement.

In the latter part of his career, he was interested in creating a profile of what a peak performer in life looked like. McClelland wanted to see if there were commonalities in what drove people from different backgrounds, different cultures, and different industries.

Through this research, my company, 2logical, had the opportunity to work in conjunction with McClelland. Collectively, we looked at more than 23,000 individuals, studying people across industries and from more than 95 different counties. At the conclusion of the study a rather startling picture began to emerge. In many ways, it was one that was somewhat counterintuitive.

For most, when they think of someone who is excelling in a given pathway in life, whether personal or professional, they tend to think that having a high level of relative skills makes the biggest difference. A salesperson becomes great because they have the highest-level selling skills. A software engineer becomes great because they have the best programming skills. A person builds great relationships because they have the best communication skills, and so forth.

However, what the research showed was a very different picture. Ultimately, there were five base-level characteristics that played a much greater role in success than someone's relative skills. What were these characteristics and to what degree do they influence our success? That's a great question.

Specific Skills — 15%

Courage Initiative — 25%

Resilience Adaptability Accountability — 60%

Based on research from Dr. David McClelland

What the researchers found is the following:

- 60% of our ability to succeed in any given endeavor will be based on how accountable, adaptable, and resilient we are. Think about it: these three characteristics are directly influenced by our belief in our *ultimate responsibility* and *limitless ability to learn*.
- 25% of our ability to succeed will be driven by our willingness to take initiative and our ability to get outside of our comfort zones and move with courage.
- 15% of our success will be driven by our relative skill sets.

What is important to note is that skill sets still matter; it is just that they play a lesser role in our success than most people think. Why is this?

Well, stop and think about it. If a person isn't accountable, they will never take ownership of learning a given skill set. If they aren't adaptable, they won't be open-minded enough to embrace the feedback necessary to learn. If they aren't resilient, they will get a negative attitude as soon as they hit the steep part of the learning curve. If they aren't willing to take the initiative, they will lack the self-motivation required to keep practicing. Last, if they are confined by their comfort zones, they will fall back into old habit patterns and never improve.

What the study showed is that skills are created by developing the right characteristics first. Our characteristics are the outgrowth of the perspective and mindset from which we approach our life.

Your Mindset Matters Most

There is one overriding common denominator among all highly successful people . . . they *think differently than everyone else.* In the most fundamental sense, their mental operating system hasn't been corrupted; as such, they move with the belief that they are *ultimately responsible* and that they have the *limitless ability to learn.* These beliefs cause them to exhibit different behaviors:

- They don't make excuses. They don't rationalize why others can succeed and they can't. They don't place blame. What they do is take ownership.
- They keep an open mind, are reflective, and believe that they can learn whatever is necessary. They recognize that each day and every endeavor is an opportunity to practice and improve.
- They stay positive in the face of adversity and challenges. They recognize that every worthwhile accomplishment is built on a foundation of obstacles overcome.
- They relentlessly focus on their dreams and goals, and this drives their self-motivation. What we think about most often is frequently what we become.
- Last but not least, they do not let fears and self-doubts stop them from acting. We all have fears, but they don't need to rule us.

(Notice that we have already begun to build these characteristics as we have been working through our rebooting process.)

The bottom line is your mindset matters far more than your circumstances. It will cause you to develop the right skill sets, to become the *right* person—the person who can recognize and then capitalize on opportunity when it presents itself.

Remember, your right place and right time is right now! So, focus on becoming the right person to capitalize on it.

Four Steps for Rebooting Your Improved Perspective

Choose an area in your life where you are struggling right now. Take a few minutes and reflect on your circumstances in this area of your life. What aspects are positive or getting better? Where do things feel like they are stalled out or getting worse? Take out a piece of paper and make a list of these two areas.

Next, considering where you feel like you are stalled out or sliding backwards. Ask yourself these questions:

1. What specific actions can I take to make forward progress?
2. What do I need to improve on in this area?
3. How can I practice this?
4. What are three things I can do today that will make my circumstances better in this area tomorrow?

Thinking "Right" Activity

Remember, our dominant thoughts shape our beliefs, and our beliefs drive our actions. Here are two affirmations that will help you make this important transition. Repeat them often in your mind.

- *I am becoming the right person to take advantage of my right place and time.*
- *Circumstances don't control my destiny; I do.*

PEOPLE–LEADER PERSPECTIVE

Waiting, wishing, and hoping is never a good strategy for success. People who are bought into the right time and right place myth give away their *ultimate responsibility* by thinking that circumstances dictate their outcomes more than their personal substance.

Before one can have, they must become. As leaders, our goal needs to be to help our people to become. We do this by stripping away the limiting beliefs (the myths) and getting people properly rooted in the truths (*ultimate responsibility and the limitless ability to learn*).

CHAPTER 13

Myth: There Is Always a Shortcut

Continuous effort—not strength or intelligence—is the key to unlocking our potential.

—Sir Winston Churchill

There is one crossroad you will come on every day. It's a subtle intersection point that, unless you are aware enough, you might miss it, walk right by, and not even notice that it's there. Yet this one point, this one transition will profoundly shape the happiness and satisfaction you find in life.

Will you succeed or suffer? Will you endeavor or simply exist? The answer to both questions lies in what you do when you reach this crossroad.

In every action that you take and in every decision you make, this crossroad will present itself. It comes into view when you must make a choice about how much effort and energy you want to expend. Do you want to just get something done as quickly as you can, with as little thought and commitment necessary? Or do you want to put forth your very best effort, strategically allocating your time and decision-making to drive toward the optimal outcome possible?

Do you want to do the *minimum* required or the *maximum* possible?

These are two distinctly different perspectives. One of them, over time, will consistently yield optimal results, whereas the other, in most cases, will lead to mediocrity.

Now, why is this true? For the simple reason that life is a marathon, not a sprint. As such, our ultimate successes or struggles will frequently come down to the positive or negative momentum we build through the decisions we make. Think of it this way: your decision and actions build momentum for the direction of your life. This is as true for bad choices as it is for good ones. Consistency can be our best friend or worst enemy when it comes to the life we lead. Remember, everything is cumulative.

DO YOUR MAXIMUMS WHERE IT MATTERS MOST

There I was sitting with one of the most financially successful people I know. He had built several companies through the course of his illustrious career, sold them, and then parlayed that success into another venture. As a result, he was able to live a lifestyle many people only dream of; he had the freedom and flexibility that financial security brings.

Looking at Bob, I couldn't help but admire his accomplishments and track record. So, one day over lunch, I made the comment, "You must be extremely proud of all that you've done."

He paused for a second, gave me a perplexed look, and said, "Not really."

Confused, I said, "How can that be? You've built four highly successful companies; you achieved a level of financial independence, most people can only wish their life looked like yours. How can you not be proud of that?"

Bob said, "Well, Dave, there's a lot you don't know. Do you know I have three kids?"

"I've never heard you mention them before, I didn't know you had a family," I said.

"Well, in the process of building those businesses, I worked really long hours. Some nights I wouldn't even bother coming home. I just slept at the office. Eventually, my wife left me and married a guy who was nowhere near as successful, but he was around, and I wasn't. My kids send me birthday and holiday cards but I don't really have much of a relationship with them; I just wasn't part of their life when they were growing up and now they don't really want to be a part of mine. I guess if I could do it all over again, I don't think I would do it the same way at all," Bob said.

That conversation happened 35 years ago, and I can still remember it like it was yesterday. I think the reason it has stuck with me was because it is such a poignant reminder of how we can spend so much time, energy, and focus chasing one thing, something that seems so important, yet in the end might not be.

Why do so many highly successful people end up with failed relationships?

This was a question I asked my mentor early on in my career. It seemed like I had met so many people who had achieved great things professionally, yet their personal lives were a disaster. Was achieving a level of success in one area of life mutually exclusive from having a happy, successful relationship with someone you care about? Does one always require you to sacrifice the other?

My mentor considered the question and replied, "People who are highly successful in their career tend to be exceptionally goal-directed and focused on accomplishing what they want. They work hard, pay their dues, and invest their time in order to get what they want. However, when they go home, many times they look at it like that's their time off, when they can put their feet up and relax. They mentally turn off and tune out in order to give themselves a break. What they often fail to recognize is the message this sends to the people at home. By being disconnected, it sends the message that they don't care and those people in their home life aren't all that important. Over time, this destroys the relationship."

Although I had never really considered this perspective, I could instantly relate. I could clearly remember times when I had spent a hectic week traveling, interacting with groups, and expending my energy trying to help other people to improve their life. Coming home, I would be tired, mentally depleted, and, candidly, a little sick of hearing my own voice. I desperately wanted to crawl into my shell, put my feet up, and mindlessly watch TV.

As I walked in the back door, the kids would come running down the hall, screaming, "Daddy's home, Daddy's home." Michelle would follow along, giving me a hug, and saying, "Why don't we go out for dinner and spend some family time together?" In my mind, the last thing I wanted was another dinner out and more restaurant food.

However, sometimes we have to consciously remind ourselves to focus on using our maximums in those areas where it most matters. Invest your time and energy in the places that are going to help you build the life that you want. You can use your minimums in the places that don't really matter that much.

Think about how you want your life to look. You don't always need to give up everything else to get what you want. Sometimes, you just need to give yourself permission to push for maximums in more than one area.

Consciously Picking Your Path

In life, what many people will chose to do is take a *minimum* approach to their actions. Thus, as they approach most things, they inherently ask themselves, "What is the minimum amount of effort that I need to put forth to get this done?" "What is the minimum amount of time I need to spend?" "What is the minimum amount of thought I need to devote?" "What is the minimum amount that I need to push and challenge myself?"

"Surely, it is better to pace myself," they think. "I should conserve my energy and effort, just in case something more important comes along." This would seem the prudent strategy, right?

The challenge is *minimums thinking* leads people to get the easiest things done first. It causes people to pursue what is fun and enjoyable over those things that are most important and impactful. It causes people to always look for the shortcut and the easiest way out. It causes people to endlessly chase instant gratification. In many cases, minimums thinking builds negative momentum.

Minimums thinking also is the fuel of every one of life's great procrastinators. After all, why put in the effort today if you can wait and do something next week, next month, or even better, next year? However, history has shown that success doesn't wait for life's procrastinators. As my mentor once told me,

"Life rewards those who take action too soon and too often, rather than too late and not enough."

As business mogul and former owner of the New England Patriots NFL team Victor Kiam once said,

"Procrastination is opportunity's assassin."

When you study those who achieve great things, what you will always find is that they have left minimums thinking far behind. They look at life and the choices before them through a different lens. As they approach situations, opportunities, and choices, they do so with a *maximums mentality*. Thinking and asking themselves, "What's the maximum benefit I can be?" What is the maximum I can learn in this situation?" "What is the maximum I can gain?" "What is the maximum I can achieve and accomplish?" "How will focusing on achieving these maximum outcomes improve my life?" "How will it create even greater opportunities for me in the future?" "What doors will open up for me?" "Who will I meet and how will they be able to help me in my journey?"

Throughout history every great endeavor, significant accomplishment, and groundbreaking invention has, without fail, been because somebody chose to take a maximums approach.

Changing Our Perspective: The Truth About Minimums Versus Maximums

Each day, billions of people wake up in the morning, crawl out of bed, try to get themselves together, put some food in their stomachs, and attempt to conquer the challenges the day will hand them. They will muddle through the day, grumbling about this and that, complaining about what ails them, and grow frustrated about what they feel they cannot control. Eventually the day grows long and evening arrives. The darkness sets in, they fall asleep, and get ready to start the whole process over again tomorrow. Day after day, week after week, month after month, and year after year, this is what their life will look like.

Through this whole process, there will be moments of joy and times of sadness; there will be laughter, sorrow, and regret. These are the signposts of life. The ratio of joy to sadness, of happiness to regret, is entirely up to you—and well within your ability to influence—as long as you make the right choices, fairly consistently. The award-winning actress Sushmita Sen once said,

> **"Life is all about choices. Everyone's destination is the same; only the paths are different."**

Making choices may seem like a daunting and somewhat overwhelming responsibility. How does one consistently make the right choices? Doesn't everyone make mistakes?

Absolutely. Rarely, if ever, is anyone 100% consistently right. We all make mistakes sometimes. It is all about the law of averages. The more "right" decisions you make, the greater the likelihood that things will work out the way you want them to.

Within all of this, there is just one overriding decision which, if you make it the right way, will have the greatest impact on your life. What is it?

Who Am I Going to Be Today?

Each day, as you roll out of bed, if you make this one simple conscious choice it will absolutely change the course of that day. Just make a firm decision regarding *who am I going to be today?*

Are you going to strive to be your best at the most important endeavors you pursue today? Or are you going to simply choose to focus on getting through the day? Realize that whichever choice you make, most consistently, will inevitably define your life.

It certainly takes less up-front effort to simply focus on getting through the day. However, just consciously acknowledge that the initial ease and comfort that comes from just existing, getting through the day, will not and cannot bring great outcomes in the future.

Conversely, it is more difficult and requires more up-front effort and energy to strive to be your best throughout the day. However, without fail, at the end of the day, you will be stronger, smarter, and better equipped than you were the day before. If you string enough of these types of days together, you will end up miles ahead in very short order.

Most of the people you will meet in life will want to pay the dues associated with taking the easy road and simply getting through the day. Yet they want the rewards that are reserved for those people who strive to be their best each day. Sadly, no matter how hard they wish this plan will work for them, it never will.

The Greek philosopher Heraclitus once said,

"Good character is not formed in a week or a month. It is created little by little, day by day. Protracted and patient effort is need to develop good character."

Willing to Pay the Dues to Be Great

As you approach each important task, ask, "What is the absolute best I can do on this?" Keep a positive attitude, ask questions, be open-minded, learn from others, get out of your comfort zone, add more things to your to-do list, have real conversations with the people around you, smile more, laugh, and engage. This is what your best looks like; recognize it, and embrace it.

Once you have lived one day as your best, back it up with another and another one after that. Bit by bit and day by day, you are developing a new habit. You are developing the habit of being your best.

Remember, everything in life is cumulative. Rarely does one thing matter; however, cumulatively things matter a great deal. So be aware that with each day you consistently focus on being your best, you are building positive momentum. Build enough positive momentum and things begin to change dramatically.

You now stand at the crossroad. The choice is yours. It will present itself to you every day, in everything that you do. Will you chase what is easiest, most fun, and immediately enjoyable right now? Are you willing to sacrifice your long-term success for the sweet taste of instant gratification? Will you take the minimums road?

Now look down the other road: it is paved with your best efforts, things that might be outside of your comfort zones, yet create incredible momentum toward your future well-being. Are you willing to push yourself? Are you willing to do your very best? Will you take the maximums road?

Make it a conscious choice. Just always remember: if you willingly pay the dues to get what you most want in life, you will be forever happier and grateful that you did.

Four Steps for Rebooting Your Improved Perspective

1. Make a list of the most important areas of your life. What are the areas of life that you are most looking to succeed in right now?
2. Choose one thing that you are going to do today to make a positive difference in one of those important areas.

3. Ask yourself: What would doing your very best at this activity look like? What attitude would you approach it with? What would you seek to learn? What outcome would you most like to achieve?
4. Make a list of the specific steps you are going to undertake today to be your best at this activity.

You can follow this same process, each and every day. Just pick the important areas of your life and consistently do the things that move your forward. Remember, consistency and effort are your best friends.

Thinking "Right" Activity

Remember, our dominant thoughts shape our beliefs, and our beliefs drive our actions. Here are two affirmations that will help you make this important transition. Repeat them often in your mind.

- *When I focus on doing minimums, I get minimums.*
- *Who am I going to be today, my maximum self or my minimum self?*

PEOPLE–LEADER PERSPECTIVE

For many people, they have never really thought about what their personal best really looks like. This is a wonderful discussion to have with both individuals and teams. Have them consider questions like these:

- What would their perfect day look like?
- What would the perfect client interaction look like?
- What would the perfect collaboration look like?
- What would the perfect project implementation look like?

With the answers to these questions in mind, it is easy to have a discussion about what specific actions the team can take to better facilitate these more perfect outcomes.

CHAPTER 14

Myth: To Succeed You Need to Be Lucky

"Good luck with that."
"Beginner's luck."
"Better luck next time."
"I'm on a lucky streak."
"Rotten luck."
"Tough luck."
"No such luck."
"As luck would have it."
"Lots of luck with that."
"The luck of the draw."
"Down on your luck."
"Better lucky than rich."
"You lucky dog."
"If it weren't for bad luck, I'd have no luck at all."
"Lucky in cards, unlucky in love."
"You should be so lucky."
"I caught a lucky break."
"He was lucky he wasn't killed!"
"I'm having nothing but bad luck."
"She's the luckiest person I know."
"Thank your lucky stars."

"Lucky for you."
"Born under a lucky star."
"With any luck."
"Don't push your luck."
"Try your luck."
"Some people have all the luck."
"He lucked into it."
"He lucked out."
"That's just my luck."
"Hard-luck story."
"A stroke of luck."
"Best of luck with that."
"You're in luck."
"A stroke of luck."
"His luck ran out."
"The luck of the Irish"
"Lady luck."
"And one for luck."
"More luck than sense."
"You lucky duck."
"You're shit out of luck."

When you take the time to consider all of the common phrases that exist in the English language containing a reference to the work *luck*, it is little wonder that so many people possess such an overriding belief in its mystical powers. In fact, most people would be hard-pressed to go through a single day without someone referring to the word *luck*. Each time we hear it, we nod our head and subconsciously buy in to the trap of thinking that our success and happiness go hand-in-hand with being lucky.

When good fortune comes, we are said to be "in luck." When the bad times befall us, our luck has "run out." If lady luck smiles, good times are ahead. If she turns her back, we might as well stay in bed because nothing is going to go right.

Society does a masterful job convincing people that the key to having the life of their dreams is all about being lucky. This belief is so powerful and pervasive that multibillion-dollar industries and entire cities are built on it. In the United States alone, we spend $80 billion a year on lottery tickets, $55 billion a year in casinos, and another $60 billion on sports betting. That's more than $200 billion per year (there are 161 countries in the world who have a GDP of less than that, so in the US alone, we gamble away more money each year than many countries make—incredible). All of this is spent on the elusive hope that luck will look favorably our way and change the course of our life.

BEING UNLUCKY ENOUGH TO WIN THE LOTTERY

Certainly luck does exist—after all, people do win the lottery, a game of chance where there is absolutely no skill involved whatsoever. It is purely random luck. However, the simple fact remains, nearly 70% of multimillion-dollar lottery winners, while lucky, will inevitably go broke. A study by the Federal Reserve Bank of Philadelphia found the vast majority of people who win a million dollars or more in the lottery will end up filing for personal bankruptcy within five years of winning.

Stop and think about that for a second. Here they are, the big lottery winner who was just handed a $10 million, $20 million, $30 million check and within five years they find themselves standing before a judge in a courthouse, filling personal bankruptcy. How crazy is that?

Now granted, it was likely one hell of a five-year run. Yet, here these lottery millionaires are five years later and in all probability they are worse off than they were before they won the lottery.

Ask yourself: Why is that? Why do you think that happens to them?

To no small extent, it's because they have broken one of the most funda-mental rules of success. We talked about it earlier in our conversa-tion, remember:

Before you can have, you must become.

These folks were lucky enough to have a $20 million check placed in their hand. However, they had never become the person who was capable of being a millionaire.

Think of all the lessons you have to learn to maintain and manage that level of wealth. To hold onto wealth, you have to learn to live within your means, stick to a budget, understand investing, be able to say no to people looking for a handout, and so on. These lottery millionaires likely hadn't developed any of these skills. They had a big check but hadn't *become* the person capable of being a millionaire.

It would seem the lottery millionaires were lucky enough to win, but they are pretty unlucky when came to holding on to their newfound wealth.

Your Success and Luck

But what about our success? What about achieving our goals and ambi-tions? What about finding happiness and peace of mind? Is that like the lottery? A game of pure chance where skill, effort, determination, and perseverance have little to no bearing. Is life really all about the luck of the draw or could something else be at play here?

When I began to study luck and its effects, I came across an interest-ing quote from Sam Goldwyn, the founder of the movie company MGM. He once said,

"It's funny but the harder I work, the luckier I seem to get."

He believed that we can manufacture our own luck through the effort we put forth. Goldwyn contended that success in life is the out-come of cause and effect, whereas winning the lottery is the out-come of luck.

Perhaps the reason people attribute success to luck is because they fail to recognize the full effort that went into creating it. After all, the media loves to highlight the outcomes, the winners, and the great successes. They can easily capture our attention with stories about the great accomplishments of people. As such, we only see the success. Rarely will the news outlets and social media platforms talk about the hard work, setbacks, mistakes, persistence, and tireless effort that it takes in order to outwardly appear lucky. The fact of the matter is, sizzle sells in the media; struggles and setbacks just aren't the sexiest of storylines.

One person who really helped me understand the science behind luck was University of Hertfordshire professor Dr. Richard Wiseman. You remember Richard, we met him earlier when we talked about how our brain is programmed to notice change. Well, through his research Richard has studied nearly 2 million people, both the lucky and the unlucky.

In one of his books, *The Luck Factor*, he set out to answer the age-old question, why do some people seem to always be luckier than others? What he found was that these people really were not any luckier; they were just quicker to spot and seize opportunities when presented with them. Their open-mindedness and the beliefs they had locked onto turned happenstance into what outwardly appears as a lucky break.

What Richard explained was that by having a higher level of focus on exactly what they were trying to achieve and working hard, these seemingly "lucky" people noticed more situations for themselves to seize opportunity. Because they are more open to life's forking paths, they are more likely to recognize the possibilities others miss. And if things don't work out the way they'd hoped, they pick themselves up, dust off the disappointment, and just keep moving forward.

One of the greatest inventors in history, Thomas Edison, once said,

"If you don't know what you are looking for, you will never know when you find it."

FOCUSING OUR BRAIN TO BRING US LUCK

In the late 1990s, my company, 2logical, and I were developing a new training program and working hard to ensure its effectiveness. Right about this time, I was fortunate enough to meet Catherine Leach. Catherine is one of the world's foremost experts in the field of adult education. She explained something to me that I have never forgotten. **Catch this: it is really important to your reboot.**

She explained that, as adults, every day we get bombarded with so much data through our five senses that if we were to become consciously aware of it all, it would short-circuit the human mind. As a result, evolution had to develop a workaround for this problem, basically a means of filtering incoming information to determine what is relevant and thus must be paid attention to, and what isn't relevant and thus can be discounted, filtered out, and therefore not noticed.

This filtering mechanism of the human mind is called our *reticular activating system* (that's a fancy name that you can use to impress your friends with). It is a central part of our survival brain. Here is how it works: Our dominant thoughts and beliefs form our referencing point for everything we experience in the world. So whenever we experience something through our five senses (sight, sound, touch, taste, or smell) that aligns with our dominant thoughts and beliefs, that input will pass through the filter of the mind and register into our conscious awareness. In other words, we have a much higher tendency to notice those things that are consistent with our dominant thoughts and beliefs.

When we experience something that is incongruent with our dominant thoughts and beliefs, these inputs have a much higher tendency to get discounted and filtered out. We tend not to notice those things that don't align with our dominant thoughts and beliefs.

Remember, evolution only cares about survival of the species. This mechanism of the mind was central to our survival. Think about it. If our ancestors believed that hungry lions were an imminent risk to their survival, they surely needed to notice when one was lurking in the weeds a few yards away. However, noticing the squirrel on the tree next to them really wasn't anywhere near as important since it posed no perceived danger, so if they didn't notice it, that really didn't matter.

Millions of years later, our brain still works this way. You notice things in your world every day, but other people around you don't notice them. Why? Because you have different dominant thoughts and beliefs than they do. You may notice that cute puppy that someone else just walked past. You may notice that creaky noise in your car that your passenger is blissfully unaware of. You may notice the stupid comments that annoying coworker makes, while someone else in the office doesn't even seem to hear them. You notice these things because they align with your dominant thoughts and beliefs.

(continued)

Because other people have different dominant thoughts and beliefs than you do, they will notice different things than you will.

The world we see and experience is entirely based on our dominant thoughts and beliefs. These determine what we notice and don't notice. This is how evolution designed us.

So what if a person has more negative dominant thoughts and beliefs? Great question; I'm glad you asked. Well, they will tend to notice more negative things in their environment, because noticing these things serves to further reinforce their negative beliefs. This becomes a vicious cycle. This is why our reboot is all about working to change flawed perspectives, eliminate those negative thoughts, and let go of the limiting beliefs. We must unbecome before we can become. If we don't, it is impossible to reboot our brain.

Changing Our Perspective: Manufacturing Our Own Luck

Through the course of my career, I have been fortunate to be able to interact with people who helped found billion-dollar startups, lead Fortune 500 companies, win Super Bowls, overcome incredible obstacles, and achieve mind-boggling accomplishments. Even though I will likely never do any of these things, just having the privilege of getting to know people who have has been a wonderful learning experience.

Over time, I began to see a common four-step pattern emerge relating to how these people were able to rise above the chaos and achieve something of magnitude in life. What I realized through all these interactions is that these people had discovered a process that enabled them to manufacture their own luck, rather than waiting and hoping something good would happen for them. The following is what I discovered.

Step 1: Willingly Pay the Dues and Put Forth the Effort

There is no shortcut to consistent effort. The time you spend and the effort you put forth create situations and circumstances in which opportunity will present itself to you. Action creates information and information teaches you how to find success. Remember, what you focus on is what you become and very likely what you will achieve.

More than 2,000 years ago, the Greek philosopher Sophocles said,

"Success is dependent on effort."

Ask yourself: What important aspect of my life am I working on right now? Am I taking enough action in this area of my life (or am I spending too much time pondering, hoping, and waiting for something good to happen)? What actions can you take today to begin to build more momentum?

Step 2: Always Be Open to New Ideas, Approaches, and Perspectives

Keep an open mind and look for the opportunities in every situation you encounter. Luck and good fortune rarely wear a billboard with neon lights exclaiming "Success Is Right Here—Pay Attention NOW!" You need to keep an open mind and be aware that success is right out there, waiting for you to find it; however, you will never see it if your eyes and mind are closed.

Author and motivational guru Zig Ziglar said,

"When you focus on problems, you get more problems. When you focus on possibilities, you get more opportunities."

Ask yourself: Who are the people in your world that could potentially help you? It doesn't matter if they aren't your best friend or a close acquaintance; most people would be honored to help you if you just ask for their advice and guidance. Look for mentors and advisors; don't let your fears keep you from making these critical connections.

Step 3: Embrace Your Setbacks; They Make You Stronger

When setbacks and disappointments come (and they will almost always come), realize that they are just part of the journey, and don't let them deter you. Every great success is built on a foundation of obstacles and setbacks that have been overcome. This reality has proven to be true time and time again. Realize that every setback is a learning opportunity in disguise, leverage it, and what you learn will be one more cinder block in the foundation of your future success. The same is true for each mistake you make; let them teach you something. Win or learn is the philosophy of "lucky" people.

Author Robert Tew said,

"The struggle you're in today is developing the strength you will need tomorrow."

Ask yourself: What's not working here? Why isn't it working? (Hint: many problems aren't externally driven; how are you complicit in your struggles? Is there an attitude or a thought process that is holding you back? What are you avoiding doing?)

Step 4: Avoid the Pseudo Experts

This is the most important step of all. Ignore the legions of "pseudo experts" and "false prophets" telling you that you can't do it. The world is full of people who would like nothing better that to include you in their club of mediocrity. If you want to be successful, if you want to be happy, if you want to be "lucky" enough to realize your dreams and ambitions, you cannot follow the same pathway that mediocre people follow. Always remember: the only good advice an unsuccessful person can give you is on how to be *unsuccessful*.

Ask yourself: Who are the people in my life who are most supportive of the direction I want to move in? Who are my naysayers and negative people? Actively work to spend more time with your supporters and protect yourself from the negative influence of the naysayers.

Thinking "Right" Activity

Remember, our dominant thoughts shape our beliefs, and our beliefs drive our actions. Here are two affirmations that will help you make this important transition. Repeat them often in your mind.

- *The harder I work, the luckier I get.*
- *With focus, perseverance, and an open mind, I can manufacture my own luck.*

PEOPLE–LEADER PERSPECTIVE

The myth of luck erodes one's belief in their *ultimate responsibility* because it places control in some unseen force that is beyond our ability to influence. Our lives are much more the outcome of cause and effect than luck. Helping employees to understand the cause and effect of their actions reinforces their belief in their *ultimate responsibility*.

Whether in one-on-one conversation or in team meetings, ask the question, What caused that to happen?

Help your people to see and understand how their thoughts and actions always drive both the positive and negative outcomes.

CHAPTER 15

Myth: Success Happens Overnight

Speak with the vast majority of people, and what you will quickly discover is that they share a common, limiting perspective about how success happens. It is a belief that has been frequently perpetuated by newspapers, magazines, television, and, more recently, it runs rampant on social media. What all these purveyors of information, these pillars of wisdom, these distributors of knowledge lead us to believe is that when success comes it comes rapidly, virtually "overnight," with little effort, with little resistance, and with little to no setbacks or obstacles.

Why is this perspective so dangerous? Because it conditions people to believe that if they try something and they're not instantaneously successful, there must be something wrong. Therefore, they should give up and quit far too soon.

In reality, success rarely if ever happens overnight. If you doubt this, just look at many of the greatest inventions, startups of iconic multibillion-dollar companies, and launching points of incredible careers. When you really do the research, you'll be hard-pressed to find a single example of a true overnight success.

It took Thomas Edison many years and more than 10,000 experiments before he was able to make the first commercially viable light bulb glow for more than a few hours. In 1878, he would use his invention to start the Edison Electric Light Company, an organization that is today known as General Electric.

It took Marie Curie more than 13 years of experimentation to isolate 1/10 of a gram of radium. This was a critical step in making x-rays possible, a discovery that would ultimately make Marie Curie the first female recipient of the Nobel Prize.

It took James Dyson 14 years and 5,127 prototypes before he was able to perfect his revolutionary vacuum cleaner. He then tried to sell the patent to every major manufacturer of vacuum cleaners and was rejected by every one of them. Ultimately, he was forced to manufacturer the vacuums himself, setting up the Dyson company. Today, Sir James Dyson is worth slightly more than $23 billion.

Henry Ford became fascinated with the idea of self-propelled vehicles in the early part of the 1890s. He built prototypes and launched four unsuccessful companies before finally realizing success with the Ford Motor Company in 1903.

As an 11-year-old girl growing up in Pakistan, Malala Yousafzai began doing humanitarian work and writing a blog about what it was like growing up under Taliban occupation. Three years later a Taliban assassin would attempt to kill her as retaliation for her activism. Despite nearly dying from a bullet wound to the head, she continued to fight until the Taliban was denounced from Pakistan. In 2014 she became the youngest Nobel Prize winner at the age of 17,

Abraham Lincoln was a failed blacksmith and general store manager. In his first attempt at running for political office he ended up finishing 8th out of 13 candidates. Ultimately, he lost in seven elections before he was finally voted in as the 16th president of the United States.

An entire book could be written (and probably has been) just highlighting all the incredible outcomes people have achieved simply because they didn't allow themselves to buy into the limiting perspective that success should happen overnight.

When looking at the most successful people, it is easy to fall into the trap of thinking that they were just geniuses who discovered a smooth pathway that rapidly led to their incredible accomplishments. However, when you study history, I mean really study the backstory, in almost every instance of great success, you will find that there was a pathway filled with setbacks, defeats, and obstacles that had to be overcome.

As a society, we only like to celebrate individuals once they have become an undeniable success. What we fail to do is highlight the tumultuous journey that they had to follow in order to seemingly emerge from nowhere overnight and awaken at the pinnacle of success.

To further compound the problem, not only does society not highlight the hardships, it frequently ridicules, criticizes, and undermines those people who are striving to accomplish something of magnitude. They're labeled foolhardy dreamers who are detached from reality, have their head in the clouds, and are wasting their life away. Their friends are all too quick to say, "Why don't you get a real job, something that will give you a steady paycheck and a viable income?" In an insidious way, this is society's way of creating accountability for a limiting perspective. Frankly, this is one of the biggest reasons why so many people swim in the sea of mediocrity their entire life.

BEING MINDFUL OF WHO IS INFLUENCING YOUR MIND

In graduate school, one of my best friends was Edward. We hung out together, double-dated with our girlfriends, even vacationed together. Many of my fondest grad school memories were hanging out with Edward.

After grad school, Edward took a job with a local company, and I decided to pursue a lifelong dream of becoming an entrepreneur. Even though our careers were on very different pathways, and we were both busy building our lives, Edward and I would still get together for dinner every other week.

More than 30 years later, I can still remember the day when my young company hit a revenue milestone. It was our first five-figure day of sales. I was over the moon, all the hard work, long hours, and sacrifice was finally starting to pay off.

That night, Edward and I were scheduled to have dinner together, and I was excited to share the good news with him. However, a few hours later as I was driving home after dinner, I was feeling melancholy and somewhat depressed. I remember thinking to myself, "It was such a great day; why am I feeling down?"

A couple of weeks later I was once again having dinner with Edward, and I found myself feeling a little depressed as I was driving back home. I began to think, "Maybe this has something to do with Edward." So I started

(continued)

to pay closer attention to our conversations over dinner and I began to see a pattern. Every time I brought up a new idea or something I was excited about, Edward would play the devil's advocate, pointing out some downside, risk, or negative aspect.

I began to think to myself, perhaps his negative perspective and cynicism wasn't really helping me. It felt like he was just planting the seed of doubt in my mind. So I slowly began to distance myself from Edward, not because I thought he was a bad person; I just thought it wasn't healthy for me or my goals to have his negativity pulling me down.

We are all surrounded by a lot of people. Most of them are good people, like Edward; they are likely well-intentioned, yet they can't help projecting their limiting perspectives on us. If we really want to be happier, more fulfilled, and successful, we not only have to reboot our brain but also we have to protect it from being undermined by people who don't have the enlightened awareness that we have.

Happiness and Success Are Often Built on a Foundation of Setbacks

As you are in the midst of your reboot and on your journey to success, recognize you will stumble. You will have setbacks. There will be times when you will be tempted to throw in the towel, to give up and quit. There will be countless opportunities to take the easy way out and no shortage of people who will try to convince you to do so.

Realize with every setback, every mistake, every time you fall and skin your knee, you are rewarded with a priceless learning opportunity. A reporter once asked inventor Thomas Edison, why he didn't give up after he at failed at thousands of attempts to invent a working light bulb. Edison gave the reporter a perplexed look and simply replied,

"I haven't failed once in my attempts to create the lightbulb; I have just discovered thousands of ways that it won't work."

Perhaps Argentine professional soccer player Lionel Messi, a man who just helped his team win the 2022 World Cup and who has been called "the best soccer player who has ever lived," summed it up best when he said,

"I started early, and stayed late, day after day, year after year. It took me 17 years and 114 days to become an overnight success."

You likely are starting to see a common theme: willingly pay the dues, suffer through the defeats, and weather the setbacks. Along the way just keep reflecting on what is working and what isn't, and learn from both.

Changing Our Perspective: Developing Persistence and Self-Motivation

The one common component in every significant accomplishment is motivation. An ever-elusive elixir that enables people to overcome challenges, work around roadblocks, and find the drive to persist in the face of every adversity, motivation is the rocket fuel of success. Those who possess it will always travel farther than those who don't.

For centuries, people have searched for, longed for, and chased what they believed was the source of motivation. People have constantly looked for that magic pill, that sage advice, or just the kick in the backside that would light a spark and propel them to success.

Entire industries have sprung up to fulfill people's insatiable desire to feel motivated. Billions are spent on self-help books, and countless people willfully invest thousands of dollars to sit at the feet of the motivational gurus hoping to learn the secret of how they, once and for all, can get out of their own way and tap into the magical force of motivation.

Yet time and again, these people come up short. Sure, they may feel inspired for a while but inevitably they slide right back to who they have always been. This externally applied motivational fix just doesn't seem to stick.

The challenge is motivation cannot be externally applied like hand lotion. It is not something that comes from a bottle, a speech given in a meeting, or from conquering some challenging activity. Motivation, sustained motivation, can only be found from one source: it can only be found within you.

The good news is self-motivation is not something that is given to some and not to others. Everyone has the ability to tap into their internal motivational driver and use it to move their life in the direction they desire.

Because this capability exists within us all, the big question becomes—how does one tap into it? How does a person find within themselves a virtual boundless well of self-motivation? Here are five simple steps that will get you started.

Step 1: Make a Decision

In 2002 the movie *8 Mile* was released. A loosely autobiographical story that detailed the evolution of a young Marshall Mathers from growing up in a poor Detroit neighborhood to selling more that 150 million rap albums and being known to the world as the musician Eminem. It was a tumultuous journey to incredible success, one fraught with setbacks and obstacles. A journey that started with one simple question, "What is it that I really want to accomplish?" Eminem once said,

> **"If people take anything from my music, it should be motivation to know that anything is possible as long as you keep working at it and don't back down."**

In 1995, a 24-year-old Stanford PhD student concluded that three evolving technologies would shape the future of humankind: the internet, energy, and space. He dropped out of school and launched his first business venture, beginning a journey that would ultimately lead Elon Musk to building a net worth of more than $200 billion. One simple question started it all: "What is it that I want to accomplish?" Elon Musk said,

> **"People should pursue what they are passionate about; that will make them happier than pretty much anything else."**

Do this: Motivation always starts with one simple decision. What is it that you truly want to accomplish? Your answer doesn't have to be grandiose. You don't have to set out to change the world, cure cancer, or discover some incredible technology. Just pick something, anything, and truly commit to making it happen.

Step 2: Embrace the Ugly Early Phase

In the early phases, success is always ugly. It's messy and looks random and unkempt. Success takes time and polishing. It is refined and beautified with time and practice. Don't allow the seemingly random nature of action and reaction to dissuade you. Keep reflecting on what is working and what's not. Keep asking yourself, what have you learned, what can you do differently, what adjustment can you make?

Thomas Edison, the most prolific inventor of all time, said,

"Opportunity is missed by most people because it is dressed in overalls and looks like work."

Do this: Be patient and embrace this ugly phase; don't get discouraged when things seem chaotic and unclear in the beginning (you should have seen the early phases of this book—*it was ugly*). With time, reflection, and refinement, the seemingly unorganized chaos begins to take shape and the pathway to success becomes clearer.

Step 3: Build Motivational Momentum

Most great accomplishments seem impossible on day one. Let's face it; if something seems impossible, what's the point in even trying? That's the attitude I had prior to my reboot. However, now you and I know better.

So hold onto your dream but focus on conquering the small steps that are immediately in front of you. Celebrate once you've made that step. Take pride in your forward progress, relish the fact that you're one small step closer. Each of these steps accumulate until you are miles ahead of where you started.

Harvard Professor Teresa Amabile said,

"Nothing is more motivating than progress."

Do this: Break your goal down into the smallest pieces possible. While it may seem overwhelming to have 100 little micro-goals, it is actually much better mentally to accomplish these small steps. It is a powerful way of showing our brain forward progress and keeping us on track.

Step 4: Create Motivational Accountability

Alone we are weak and easily defeated. Setbacks and negative thinking can quickly take root and steal away our motivation. Selectively sharing our ambitions with supportive people makes a huge difference.

When no one is around to say anything about our lack of progress, it's easy to fall victim to procrastination and the distractions of life. Conversely, having someone there to congratulate us on our progress or kick us in the pants when we are dragging our feet keeps us focused and motivated.

Do this: Pick an accountability buddy, someone who is a positive force in your life and who wants the very best for you. Share your goals and plans with this person. Let them know the deadlines you have set and ask for their help in holding you accountable to them. It is amazing how much of a difference this small step can make. Businesswoman and TV personality Oprah Winfrey said,

"Surround yourself with people who are going to lift you higher."

Step 5: Surround Yourself with a Motivational Mastermind Group

Rarely does one person possess all the wisdom and insights required to succeed. Although they certainly can learn, there is a shortcut to this process.

In the early 1900s, author Napoleon Hill wrote about the value of bringing together people from varying backgrounds and experiences to collectively focus on coming up with ideas and solutions. He coined this a *mastermind group*.

Throughout history, notable achievers have all leveraged this mastermind principle to expedite their success. Benjamin Franklin, Thomas Edison, Marie Curie, Orville and Wilbur Wright, Andrew Carnegie, Oprah Winfrey, and even Jesus all surrounded themselves with a small group of people who helped them to vet problems and see new perspectives. If this strategy can work for these luminaries, it certainly can work for us. Noted cultural anthropologist Margaret Mead once said,

"Never doubt that a small group of thoughtful committed citizens can change the world; indeed, it's the only thing that ever has."

Within you and each of us exists everything necessary to succeed. The passion, the purpose, the motivation, and the drive required to build a meaningful life; it's all there, waiting for you to tap into it. You may not have always seen or felt this; however, that doesn't mean it's not there. Many times there is a multiplicative impact when we bring a group together that helps lift our spirits, perspectives, and will.

Do this: Pick a group of people who are looking to accomplish something in their lives. (They don't all need to be looking to accomplish the same thing; they just need to be positive, forward-thinking individuals.) Bring these people together and share with them your idea of creating a mastermind group to help one another move forward in life. Set a regular time to meet. In each meeting, have each person share their forward progress and setbacks. Provide thoughts to one another regarding the lesson contained within the setbacks. Last but not least, at the end of each session, have every member set a goal or objective that they want to have accomplished by the next mastermind meeting.

Thinking "Right" Activity

Remember, our dominant thoughts shape our beliefs, and our beliefs drive our actions. Here are two affirmations that will help you make this important transition. Repeat them often in your mind.

- *Each setback makes me stronger, smarter, and one step closer to success.*
- *There are no unrealistic goals, just unrealistic time frames.*

PEOPLE–LEADER PERSPECTIVE

Outlandish expectations and a sense of entitlement oftentimes foster disillusionment and a lack of engagement. Helping people to have more realistic expectations of the time and investment required to achieve their desired level of success helps them to more willingly pay the necessary dues.

To aid your team in their journey, set up a team mastermind group. Bring this group together on a consistent basis to share their successes and setbacks. Encourage them to share ideas, insights, and lessons learned. (Hint: resist the urge to always be the one speaking. Let the group carry the discussion. You will be much more effective guiding the conversation by just using insightful questions.)

Leveraging this mastermind process will build comradery, lessen the sting of losses, and greatly accelerate everyone's growth.

CHAPTER 16

Super Myth: Failure Should Be Avoided

What if the one thing you avoided most, something you dreaded and feared, was really one of the most important parts of succeeding?

Most people hate the very idea of failure. They loathe the prospect of thinking of themselves as coming up short, missing the mark, and not succeeding. For many, just the possibility of failure is enough to convince themselves that it is not even worth trying. They think to themselves, isn't it better to set the bar lower, keep my expectations in check, and minimize the risks I'm taking?

Certainly, playing it safe is a great strategy if your job requires defusing bombs or performing brain surgery. Yet for most of us, in most situations, the negative ramifications of failure are really relatively minor. After all, wouldn't you be willing to fall down, skin your knee, and screw something up if you knew for certain that you would succeed in the end? In fact, isn't this the exact reason you walk around each day?

If you take the time to journey back in the history books and really study success, you will find that there is one common thread woven into every story of accomplishment. It is one of people failing their way to success.

At the age of 21, Rowland Macy opened a small retail store in Haverhill, Massachusetts. It was his first of seven failed business attempts. With each failed venture, he learned, adjusted, and adapted his understanding of what was required to make a business succeed. Finally after

15 years of trying, he dialed in the right combination and founded the Macy's Department Store, a retail institution that has stood for more than 150 years.

The oft-quoted, Nobel Prize–winning Winston Churchill suffered from a debilitating lisp, struggled in school, and nearly died after falling 29 feet off a bridge at the age of 18 (likely because he was drunk). He lost in numerous elections and suffered staggering political failures before finally being elected Great Britain's prime minister at the ripe old age of 62.

Author J. K. Rowling battled depression and struggled in abject poverty as a single mother. Then one day while waiting for a delayed train, she came up with the idea for the character of Harry Potter. For five years, she toiled away, writing as time would permit. Finally, she finished her manuscript and sent it off to various publishers. She received one rejection after another. In total, 12 different publishers all passed on her book. Yet she persisted until one agreed to do a small run of 1,000 books. Little did they realize that the Harry Potter series would capture the imagination of so many people. To date, the series has more than 500 million books in print and J. K. Rowling, the single mother who at one point in her life was forced to go on welfare, is today a billionaire.

As we've discussed, the pathway to success is never a smoothly paved road. Those who think that happiness, fame, riches, and greatness come without resistance, setbacks, and obstacles are only setting themselves up for disappointment and disillusionment.

Changing Our Perspective: Making Failure Our Friend

So, what is the key? How can you make failure your friend and leverage it to build the life that you desire?

Step 1: Fail More Frequently

Thomas Watson, the founder IBM, was once asked what his key to success was. He said,

"It's simple; just double your rate of failure."

If you are never failing, own up to the fact that you're not trying hard enough. Staying in your comfort zone and playing it safe is the surefire way to find the sea of mediocrity. Start experimenting and trying new things. Recognize that some will work out and some won't; that is how it is supposed to be. Embrace that fact.

Don't be afraid to try. Doing something "too soon" and "too often" will always serve you better than doing something "too late" and "not enough." And always remember, the worst possible thing is *doing nothing*.

Do this: Ask yourself three questions:

- What do I want my life to look like this month? (Setting a shorter-term picture helps build our belief system and keeps us on track. Be realistic: in the next month, you likely aren't going to win the lottery, become a billionaire, or star in the next Tom Cruise movie. Sorry, you may need to let those dreams go for now. What can you really make the next month look like?)
- Who do you want to work on becoming this month? What skills and abilities do you want to learn? How can you practice these things?
- What specific steps can you take each day to move your life in the right direction? Don't be fazed if some of these steps don't work out. (Remember, fail frequently. It is better to try something, have it not work out, and then learn from it than to do nothing and learn nothing.)

Think about each of these questions. Your answers will define everything for you in life. If you're uncertain, keep thinking about it.

Step 2: Fail Faster

Albert Einstein once said,

> **"The definition of insanity is doing the same thing over and over and expecting to get a different result."**

Sadly, many people fall into the insanity trap of repeating flawed actions over and over again almost every day. They do this for one simple reason: they aren't asking themselves the right questions.

Taking the time to look at your life. Just asking, what's working? and what's not working? is critical. Reflection is one of our most powerful (and often underused) tools. Most people sprint through their days without taking a single moment to reflect on how effective (or ineffective) they are.

Do this: Twice a day, set aside time to reflect. Block it out on your schedule if you have to; it's that important. (Hint: I've found that what works best for me is to set aside a few minutes right before lunch and right before I go to sleep at night). Ask these questions at every reflection point:

- What's working? What am I doing right, right now?
- What's not working? What am I doing wrong, right now? What have I been avoiding doing?
- What am I learning? What adjustments can I make? How can I do it better moving forward?

If something isn't working, if it is not serving you, if it's not helping you move your life in the direction you desire, change it. Fail fast and make the adjustments necessary. The legendary motivational speaker Zig Ziglar had a wonderful saying,

> **"If you have to kiss a frog, kiss it quickly; it's not going to get any prettier."**

Don't linger with something that is failing; acknowledge it and try approaching it from a different direction.

Step 3: Fail Forward

Retired naval aviator and bestselling author Denis Waitley once said,

> **"Failure should be our teacher, not our undertaker. Failure is a delay, not a defeat. It is a temporary detour, not a dead end. Failure is something we can avoid only by saying nothing, doing nothing, and being nothing."**

WISE WORDS FROM AN UNLIKELY SOURCE

The three of us were driving in Rhode Island from one city to another. It had been a long day of meetings, and we were all looking forward to getting to our next hotel and winding down from the day.

We stopped at a gas station to fill up, and the guy who was sitting in the back seat goes into the store and walks out with a six-pack of beer. As we resumed our trip, he proceeds to crack open one beer after another and begins rambling away as intoxicated people have a tendency to do.

Then all of a sudden, he spits out the following phrase:

"I've always tried to look at life as a win-or-learn proposition."

As I sat there in the front seat, I reflected on those words, I realized that was a very profound statement to flow from the mouth of a drunk.

So often we look at life as a succeed-fail, win-lose proposition. Although this thought process does apply to competitive sports, it really doesn't translate well to everyday life.

In our day-to-day existence, the only way that we can truly fail is if we never try or if we quit trying. As long as we keep moving forward and keep learning along the way there are only two options that lay before us: we succeed or we die trying. No matter what we do, we are going to die at some point (hopefully later rather than sooner). So what is the downside to using our time to pursue greater happiness, joy, success, wisdom—what risk are we really taking by pursuing whatever we desire?

Life truly is a win-or-learn proposition.

Once you come off a playing field in sports, life isn't about winning or losing. Life is about winning or learning. If you approach the concept of failure from a win–or–learn perspective, you quickly recognize there is no downside. If you set out to do something and you accomplish it— you have won. If you fail to accomplish it, you have the opportunity to learn something that will help you win next time.

If every failure teaches a valuable lesson that moves you forward, closer to what you want, how can failure be looked at as a bad thing or something to be avoided? Isn't making progress highly desirable? Isn't it exactly what you want to be doing each day? Failure is actually your friend, not an enemy who should be avoided at all cost.

Always remember, the greatest benefit of failure is the priceless learning opportunities that it provides. Rather than hiding from your failures, sweeping them under the rug and ignoring them, study and learn from them. Your failures will provide you with a PhD in how to succeed.

Do this: Ask yourself, "What am I failing at right now?" (If your answer to that question is I'm not failing at anything, you're either lying to yourself, not trying hard enough, or you should be authoring this book, not me.) Face facts: we are all struggling with something, somewhere in our life. Some aspect of our life isn't quite where we want it to be. Don't pretend it is all right; own up to it. You can't fix something unless you first admit to yourself it isn't working.

Next, ask yourself, "What is it that I am doing (or not doing) that is contributing to my struggles in this area?" This is an incredibly insightful question, so be honest with yourself. Frequently, we are our own worst enemy and we don't even realize it. Based on the insights you gain from this question, fail forward by identifying specific things you can learn or do to make things better.

Step 4: Say Farewell to Your Failures

Richard Branson, billionaire entrepreneur and founder of more than 400 companies under his flagship Virgin brand, said it well,

"In order to grow, you must let go."

Recognize that failure is a temporary state, a tollbooth you must pass through on the road to bigger and better things. Failure doesn't define you, nor should it confine you. Don't linger with or label yourself based on your failures. They are nothing more than a reflection of your actions, not your self-worth. You can always change your actions to get a better outcome.

If something didn't work out, accept it, learn from it, adjust based on what you've learned, and then let go of what happened yesterday. It is your past, not your present or your future. Remember, your very best days, your brightest hours, your greatest achievements will be built on the failure that you said farewell to yesterday.

Do this: Keep reminding yourself of where you want to go, who you want to become, and what you want to do. Most people spend far too many of their days living in the past holding onto bad memories (and replaying them over and over). I spent the better part of 50 years doing this and I can assure you, it will bring you nothing but dissatisfaction, heartache, and unhappiness. Your best days are today and what will follow. Don't allow the issues of the past to cast shade on the sun that is shining today. Don't allow your past to eclipse your future.

Thinking "Right" Activity

Remember, our dominant thoughts shape our beliefs, and our beliefs drive our actions. Here are three affirmations that will help you make this important transition. Repeat them often in your mind.

- *Every setback teaches me how to succeed as long as I allow it to.*
- *The only true failure is to never try or to quit trying.*
- *Every day, I win or I learn.*

PEOPLE–LEADER PERSPECTIVE

In virtually every organization my company, 2logical, goes into, employees exhibit a high level of risk aversion, a desire to avoid making mistakes, and a reluctance to try new things. Each of these issues offers the perception of the possibility to fail. If failure is deemed as the ultimate negative, then it is little wonder that organizations find it so difficult to drive change.

Highly successful leaders create an environment of psychological safety for their people. In this type of environment, it is not only okay to make a mistake, but also encouraged—as long as learning happens. As leaders, we can mitigate the risk level; however, if the environment and culture is intolerant of mistakes, it is also intolerant of learning, adjusting, and adapting.

Let your people know that you have their back if they make a mistake. Help them see that mistakes are inherent in the learning process and learning is the most important part of success.

Also, don't be afraid to humanize yourself by sharing some of the mistakes you have made and the important lessons you gained from them.

(Hint: how you react when someone comes to you regarding a mistake they made is critically important. If you remain calm and patient, it sends a powerful message. Focus on helping the person fix the mistake and learn a lesson, not on belittling or second-guessing them. Remember, they are likely already beating themselves up; they don't need your help with that.)

CHAPTER 17

Super Myth: Feedback Can Be Negative

Are you a good person or a bad person?

This seemingly simplistic question was asked of me more than 30 years ago by my mentor, Joe Gianni. Without much reflection, I answered, "A good person."

At the time I didn't really understand the ramifications or ripple effect of my response. In fact, it has taken more than three decades to really wrap my head around it.

Now, I want to ask you that same question: "Are *you* a good person or a bad person?"

Take a moment and really ponder that question. Think about it before you just give an offhanded response.

Certainly you've made mistakes in your life; you've said and done things you regret (we all have; it's okay, that's part of being human; we are all inherently flawed and make mistakes). However, do your past mistakes make you a fundamentally bad person? At your core, are you a good person or a bad person?

Likely you aren't some evil-doer, criminal mastermind, or a serial killer (and if you are, you certainly need a brain reboot—so keep reading). For most of us, at our core we are good people. Yes, we are flawed, carry emotional baggage, and sometimes do stupid things, but deep down, we are still a good person.

Go ahead, say it out loud, "I am a good person." Go ahead, say it again. It feels good to say it, doesn't it? This is probably a good thing to remind yourself of now and again.

Why it is so important to consciously make this determination?

Well, have you ever made a mistake and had that little voice in your head (you know that one we talked about earlier, that little voice that lives in our solver/critical brain), say something like, "Oh, you're such an idiot, why did you do that?" (I know I've heard that phrase many times echoing through my brain.)

So often, that little voice in our head is negative, critical, judging, belittling, and reinforcing all of our perceived shortcomings. It is giving us feedback that's attacking the core of who we are. It is telling us that because we screwed up, we are a bad person. Well, that little voice is lying to us.

Sometimes we take bad actions, but that doesn't make us a bad person. We can change our actions. We're still a good person.

Have you ever been in conversation with someone, a friend, coworker, or family member, and this person starts giving you some feedback? They're telling you something that they think you're doing wrong or screwing up. In these moments, have you ever felt your defense mechanisms rising up? Emotions like anger, resentment, frustration, fear, and disgust frequently come over us in these instances. Have you experienced this as well? (I know I've been in this place many, many times in my life.)

It feels like that person is attacking us, somehow undermining us, or telling us that we are fundamentally flawed. It feels like they are telling us that we're a bad person. But are they really? Or are they just trying to let us know that the actions we've been taking aren't working?

Why does the internal feedback from our inner voice and the external feedback from those around us feel so bad? Why does it make us feel defensive and on guard? Why does it feel belittling and demeaning?

It was Dr. Christina Hibbert who helped me to understand why. Christina is a clinical psychologist and author who was been called one of the most inspirational healthcare professionals in the United States. Here is what I came to understand from her.

Most of us have been conditioned to attach feedback to our sense of self-worth. Certainly a pat on the back, a thank-you, or a "good job" feels nice, right? We like the positive feedback, the recognition. It builds us up because it enhances our sense of self-worth and self-esteem.

The inverse is also true. When someone says something about us that isn't so flattering, when they are critical of us or tell us we screwed something up—boom!—it feels like a body blow right to our sense of self-worth. That's why we run from the negative feedback, avoid it, deny it, or outright ignore it. Anytime we get anything less than glowing feedback it feels like a personal attack.

So what. Why does this matter? Why can't we just move through life constantly seeking the glowing praise of others or the feel-good comfort of false self-satisfaction. What's wrong with drinking up all the good stuff and ignoring the bad?

Aren't we supposed to avoid bad stuff? Isn't that kind of key to survival? I mean, we avoid bullets, bombs, and bankruptcy, and that seems like it has worked out for us, right?

On the surface this may make sense. However, I want to bring you back to a question I asked before. From what have you learned more: your successes or your setbacks? Now be honest with yourself here. What's been your better teacher: your successes or your setbacks?

Yup, you got it. You and I learn very little from our successes. However, we learn a ton from our setbacks. But only if we will allow ourselves to embrace the feedback. Seek it out, even.

Remember what we learned earlier in our conversation: feedback is the fuel of our subconscious mind; it is how we learn, refine, and improve. Without it, we never would have survived as a species. Not being willing to learn from their mistakes would have quickly extinguished our ancestors. A willingness to embrace and learn from feedback has gone hand-in-hand with every advancement in humankind.

CONSIDER THE MESSAGE MORE THAN THE SOURCE

My son Ben was playing travel soccer as a kid. One day he comes home from practice and tells me, "Dad, I don't wanna play soccer anymore." "How come?" I asked. "Well, coach is always yelling at us; I'm sick of getting yelled at all the time."

"I can understand that. Let me ask you: what was he yelling about today?" "I don't know; he just kept yelling," Ben said. "Well, stop and think about it for a minute; what specifically was he yelling about?"

(continued)

Ben thought for a minute and said, "Well, he was yelling because we weren't playing our positions and passing the ball enough." I said, "Okay, was he right?" "I don't know, I'm just sick of getting yelled at," Ben said. "I understand that; however, was he right? Were you guys not playing your positions and not passing enough?" "Probably," he grudgingly admitted.

I explained to him that in life there are going to be a lot of times where someone will be giving him feedback. Sometimes he might not like the feedback and sometimes he might not like the way it was being delivered. However, that shouldn't automatically cause him to discount the value of the feedback.

Many times, if people don't like the feedback they are receiving, especially if it is true, they will look for a reason to discount the messenger. Metaphorically, if they can kill the messenger, their feedback dies with them.

Yes, not all feedback is valid. Before accepting someone's feedback we should ask ourselves two critical questions.

First, does this person have specialized knowledge regarding the subject matter they are advising us on? (After all, people who have been divorced five times really shouldn't be doling out marital advice—unless of course they are advising you on how to get divorced; they would seem to be an expert in that.)

Second, is this person 100% committed to helping you to achieve your goals and ambitions? (If your agendas are aligned and this person has consistently shown that they have your best interests at heart—listen. If they are working another agenda and trying to manipulate you for their purposes, be very wary of their feedback.)

Changing Our Perspective: Making All Feedback Positive (Even the Bad Stuff)

Remember: you're a good person. Good people make mistakes. Mistakes happen when our actions lead to undesirable outcomes. Every time this happens, we are given a golden opportunity to learn from those actions to adjust and refine so that our next action is more effective. Simple as that.

So how can feedback be bad or negative if it helps us to improve? Is improvement undesirable? Is getting better and more effective a bad thing? No, of course not. Just as failure is our friend, so, too, is feedback.

Really, the only time feedback can be classified as bad or negative is when one of the following happens:

- The person giving it to us has bad intentions or lacks the level of expertise necessary to be able to share valuable insights. (An idiot can only advise on how to be an idiot; that's where their expertise ends.)
- When we use it to beat ourselves up, undermine our self-confidence, and weaken our resolve. If we weaponize feedback and attack ourselves with it, then feedback is worthless. What good does it do if we take our mistakes and use them to mentally beat the snot out of ourselves? All it does is make us feel bad and second-guess ourselves next time. All pain and no gain.

Do this: Actively work to seek out feedback. Look for it in every important thing that you do. Ask for it if it isn't offered. Immerse yourself in a sea of feedback. When feedback is valid, more of it is always better than less of it. Remember, feedback feeds your future success. As such, don't run from feedback; feast on it.

Thinking "Right" Activity

Remember, our dominant thoughts shape our beliefs, and our beliefs drive our actions. Here are three affirmations that will help you make this important transition. Repeat them often in your mind.

- *Feedback is the breakfast of champions.*
- *Feedback is my friend because it helps me learn and makes me better.*
- *Every day I seek feedback, it fuels my success.*

PEOPLE–LEADER PERSPECTIVE

In many organizations leaders seem reluctant to give feedback. Partially this is driven by two factors: (1) sometimes employees respond to feedback in less than optimal ways (defensiveness, anger, high emotion levels, and so on), which drives (2) leaders to become uncomfortable providing anything but glowing feedback.

(continued)

Yet, we understand that feedback (all feedback) is essential to assisting our subconscious minds in developing new and better plans to execute on. As leaders we must work to help employees view feedback not as a personal assault to their sense of self-worth but rather a tool to help them to grow and improve.

Creating a high feedback environment where successes, setbacks, wins, and losses are studied and analyzed is critical to the team's success and employee growth.

A great strategy is to integrate reflection into both team meetings and one-on-one conversations. Use the reflection questions we discussed previously to guide these conversations:

- What did you do right? What worked well and why did it work?
- What did you do wrong or avoid doing? Knowing what you know now, what would you do differently?
- What were the key takeaways or lessons you can use to be even more successful moving forward?

These are the most important questions you will ever ask as a leader. When you leverage them frequently enough, you begin to recondition your people in a way that causes them to break feedback away from their sense of self-worth. Feedback becomes about learning, not judgment. This is one of the most important transitions a leader can make with their team.

CHAPTER 18

Super Myth: You Should Be Afraid of Fear

There exists one word in the English language, a simple four-letter word that has the power to conquer virtually everything it encounters. Throughout the ages it has wreaked more havoc, destroyed more dreams, and crippled the actions of more people than any natural disaster that Mother Nature has ever thrown at us. What is this almighty four-letter word? *Fear.*

The root of every excuse, every rationalization, and every justification can ultimately be traced back to fear. The philosopher and poet Suzy Kassem once said,

"Fear kills more dreams than failure ever will."

Fear robs us of our will. It convinces us the risks are too great and the probability of success is too low. Fear plants the seed of doubt, and once it takes root, it kills most everything it comes into contact with. Fear truly does kill more dreams than failure ever will for the simple reason that fear convinces people not to try. If they don't try, they will never fail; however, they will also never succeed.

Ironically, most of what we fear never comes to fruition. In a study at the University of Pennsylvania it was found that 91.4% of all fears didn't come true. I mean, would you go to a surgeon who had a 91.4% failure rate? Would you fly on an airline that crashed 91.4% of the time?

No way. Yet we trust our fears like they are the word of God. If our fears are wrong so much of the time, why do we possess this debilitating emotion and why do we place so much faith in it?

Well, if you follow the logic of evolution, fear is likely our oldest emotion. The reason fear proceeded all other emotions is simply because it is the one emotion that is most closely tied to survival of the species (remember, survival is the only thing evolution truly cares about).

Fear made our ancestors wary of walking into darkened caves. Fear made them avoid growling predators. Fear kept our ancestors from walking off cliffs. Fear kept our ancestors alive long enough to procreate and perpetuate the species. To no small extent, fear is the reason you and I are here today.

In its earliest iterations, fear served a very noble purpose. Millions of years ago, it was essential to survival of the species.

However, a lot has changed in the last 10 million years. Rarely do we have the opportunity to walk into dark caves. We are no longer in the middle of the food chain. Just stop and ask yourself: when was the last time you heard of a human being stalked and eaten by a hungry predator? Doesn't really happen all that often now, does it?

Our environment today is not so danger laden as that of our ancestors. Simply put, there just aren't as many things out there trying to kill us as there used to be. So what impact has this had on us as a species? As the risks of our environment lessened, did our fears go away? Did they dissipate? Absolutely not! Fear lives in us just as much as it did our ancestors. The primordial emotion of fear still exists; it still rules us on a daily basis. It is woven into our DNA.

THE HIDDEN PROFITABILITY OF FEAR

Earlier in our conversation, we talked about the six universal emotions that live in our communicator brain: fear, anger, disgust, sadness, surprise, and happiness. These are the six root emotions that evolution handed us to perpetuate the survival of the species. These emotions create a negative bias in the brain that exists to help protect us from harm.

What you may not realize is how these emotions are oftentimes used to manipulate your behaviors. Let me explain.

Have you ever noticed the negative bias that exists in the news media? Just turn on any of the 24-hour cable news networks. It doesn't matter which one you pick—watch for a few moments, and just notice the ratio of negative news to positive news. What you'll quickly pick up is that there is a lot more negative news. This isn't by accident.

The psychologists who advise cable network executives understand what you and I understand. They know how evolution designed the human mind to have a negative bias. They realize that our brain is programmed to put more emphasis on and pay more attention to negative inputs. It was this function of our brain that helped protect our ancestors from harm. It is this aspect of the brain that is now used against us.

Here's how. The cable news networks understand that if they pump out more negative news, our brain will cause us to pay closer attention; we will watch for longer periods of time. The longer we watch, the more commercials we will see. The more commercials we watch, the more money they make.

Each year, corporations make billions of dollars leveraging our fears against us. Politicians run negative campaigns to get themselves elected to office. Social media companies use the fear of missing out, also known as FOMO, to draw us back to their platforms, and then encourage people to share images of themselves "living their best life," which makes other users fear that their life will never measure up. Just look around you: fear and negativity run rampant. Why? Because it is one of the easiest ways to manipulate human behavior.

It was Susan Forward who really helped me understand how easily we can be emotionally manipulated. Susan has a PhD in psychology and is a bestselling author who has done a tremendous amount of research in this area. She explained that fear, obligation, and guilt are the three most targeted emotions used by people whose goal is psychological manipulation. Fear plays to our most root survival instincts and thus triggers our motivational intelligence, and obligation and guilt play to our communal and social instincts, thus triggering our emotional intelligence.

Fear, obligation, and guilt are the most profitable emotions of all time. They have been used for centuries to move nations of people in a given direction, inspire wars, influence behaviors, or get us to open our wallets and spend money.

(continued)

The challenge with all of this is, over time, we begin to feel like we are drowning in a sea of negativity. It starts to feel immersive. Everywhere we go we feel more vulnerable, we feel more wary of that stranger walking down the road, more at risk as we move through our day-to-day lives, and more like our lives will never be as "great" as those of other people. As the tools of manipulation have become more sophisticated and prevalent, this has caused the rates of anxiety and depression to skyrocket. The World Health Organization reports a 25% increase in just 2022 alone.

However, once we are aware, as you now are, you can protect yourself from the manipulation. You get to choose what you pay attention to. You get to choose if you want to allow people to manipulate you for profit or political gain. Choose what and whom you pay attention to wisely. It has a much bigger ripple effect on your happiness than most people realize.

The Changing Role of Fear

As human beings, we began to domesticate animals and grow crops about 12,000 years ago. Roughly 3,000 years ago, we began to build civilizations with small cities, roadways, and create roles for labor and governments. In the last 300 years, we've seen the rise of industrialization, which has brought with it bigger cities, centralized manufacturing, mass transportation, and large-scale agriculture. However, the single biggest change that has happened in human existence has occurred over the last 50 years with the rise of technology. It has transformed every aspect of how we live our lives today.

Through all of these changes in how we live our lives, the nature of fear has also transformed. Our fear of physical harm and mortal danger is largely perpetuated through the media; however, statistically it is very unlikely. Today, our fears are much more tied to the prospect of psychological risk rather than physical risk.

What if I do this and it doesn't turn out right? What if I screw this up? What if I mess up this project? What if I forget what I'm going to say in this big presentation? What if I embrace this new strategy and it doesn't work? What if I make a fool out of myself? What if this new change in the way we are doing things means something bad for me? What if I lose my job? What if my partner leaves me? What if they say no?

What if? Perhaps the scariest question for many people. TV personality and psychologist Phil McGraw (aka Dr. Phil) once said,

"80% of all choices are based on fear. Most people don't choose what they want, they choose what they think is safe."

Anytime there is a perception of psychological risk, people can't help but consider the possible negative outcomes. Will they feel stupid? Will they look foolish in front of their peers? Will their boss yell at them? Will they get fired? Will they get rejected? All of these are unknowns. Unknowns inspire our emotion of fear. Fear paralyzes people from taking action.

Interestingly, as babies, most researchers agree, we are born with only two innate fears: the fear of falling from high heights and the fear of loud noises. These are survival fears that were woven into our DNA over millions of years.

Most of the things adults are afraid of inspire absolutely no fear response in children. Babies aren't afraid of the water; after all, they lived for nine months suspended in amniotic fluid. Nor are they claustrophobic. Babies actually find comfort in tightly confined spaces because it reminds them of the time when they were safely tucked away in their mother's womb.

The fear of failure. The fear of change. The fear of public speaking. The fear of rejection. The fear of judgment. The fear of ridicule. The fear of dying. Even the ever-present fear of creepy crawly things (spiders, snakes, bugs, and other little critters)—every one of these anxiety-causing, gripping fears we were not born with; we had to learn to be afraid these things.

So, we all have fears, and once engrained, they do not go away. However, we can decidedly influence the degree to which our fears debilitate us. In fact, one of the biggest differences between happy and fulfilled people and those who struggle in life is learning to rule your fears rather than be ruled by your fears. Nelson Mandela once said,

"I learned that courage was not the absence of fear, but the triumph over it. The brave person is not the one who doesn't feel afraid, but rather the one who conquers that fear."

BECOMING COMFORTABLE WITH THE IDEA OF BEING UNCOMFORTABLE

As I was coming out of graduate school, similar to all my peers, I was interviewing for jobs and trying to figure out my next steps in life. I interviewed with the big money–center banks, Wall Street investment firms, and large consulting companies. I was chasing the dream of a six-figure starting salary and a life of financial prosperity.

After what felt like hundreds of interviews, I was coming close to taking a job with a major Wall Street firm as an investment banker. It looked like a great opportunity for launching my career, yet something didn't feel quite right, and I couldn't quite put my finger on what it was.

As I was considering my future and about ready to accept this position, I found myself sitting with one of my professors, Bob Barbato. I was sharing with him my concerns and reservations and looking for his advice and guidance.

I'll never forget what he asked me. "Dave, if you could do anything in your career, anything at all, what would you do?"

I sat and thought about that question and said, 'Well, my dad was an entrepreneur. As long as I can remember, he has run his own business. I guess if I could do anything, I would really like to have my own business."

"So, why don't you do that? Why don't you start your own company?" Bob asked.

"For starters, I don't know what type of company I would start. I don't really have any business idea of what would my company do. How would it make money? For that matter, I don't have any money to start a company with." On and on I went with a litany of reasons why I couldn't start a business.

Bob sat patiently as I went through my list of excuses and then he shared with me one of the best pieces of wisdom I have ever received. "Dave, over the course of your life there are going to be a lot of things that you're going to want to do. You'll gather all the facts, do all the research, and try to cover all your bases. Even still, you'll get to a point where it feels like you are standing at the edge of a cliff."

"As you're standing at that mental cliffside, you'll look over the ledge and see all the unknowns, all the uncertainties, all the negative possibilities of what could happen if you move forward. Then you'll look back over your shoulder at the relative safety and security of your known. It will feel like if you turn around and walk away from that cliff, there will be less perceived risk, a seemingly lower chance of making a mistake and failing."

"What I've found is that when you're in that situation, most people will turn and walk away from the ledge of that mental cliff, rather than take a chance. Me, I've always taken the forward step."

"What I discovered is that what seemed like a mountainous cliff in my mind was really an imaginary line in the sand. More important, everything I truly value in my life, everything that has really enhanced my life and made me feel complete, I have found by making that forward step."

That afternoon, I went home and called that Wall Street investment bank and told them that I was no longer interested in their position. I also began to do the research, gather the facts, and gain the insights necessary to start my first business. My entire life changed that afternoon.

Many times throughout my life, I have stood at the edge of that imaginary cliff looking over and wondering if I should just turn around and walk away. Then I remember Bob's sage advice and make the forward step. Everything that really means something to me in my life has been found on the other side of that imaginary line in my mind.

What are your cliffs? How can your life change, for the better—forever, if you allow yourself to become comfortable with the idea of being uncomfortable and make that forward step?

Changing Our Perspective: Becoming Comfortable with Being Uncomfortable

Our comfort zones are an imaginary boundary line that exist in the mind. Similar to all lines, they have two anchoring points. The first anchoring point of our comfort zones will be based on our current level of experience. Any time we are looking to do something that we have never done before, we will bump into our comfort zones. We will feel that sense of apprehension and trepidation. We will start to sweat and the emotion of fear will rise up.

The second anchoring point of our comfort zones is based on our belief in our potential. Any time we are considering doing something that we are uncertain we can be successful at, once again our comfort zones, fears, and anxieties will rise up.

It is important to understand that these are natural human responses. Recognize these feelings, don't deny and hide from them; rather, embrace them. Realize that everything you value most, the things you cherish and are proud of, most likely all came into being because at one moment in time you gave yourself permission to step outside of your comfort zone. All success, all greatness, and a lot of our happiness happens on the other side of our comfort zones.

Get comfortable with the idea of being uncomfortable. When you feel that sense of apprehension rising, in most cases, it is because you are doing something that is going to make you better, happier, stronger, and more successful. The great poet Ralph Waldo Emerson once said,

"Those who are not every day conquering some fear have not learned the secret of life."

Learning to override your fears unshackles you and empowers you to build a better, more fulfilled, and happier life. So the critical question is, how does one move past their fears, overcome self-doubts, and find the courage to take the actions that will ultimately lead to their success?

The good news is, courage is not something that is born to some and not to others. Similar to self-motivation, courage exists within all of us; we just need to understand how to draw it out. So here are *three simple strategies* to help you draw on your limitless well of courage and leverage it to overcome your fears.

Step 1: Get to Know Your Unknowns

What lurks in the deep recesses of the dark closet is scary. We don't like things that we can't see; we can't prepare and protect ourselves from them. Thus, we avoid them in an effort to perpetuate our own existence and mental well-being.

However, should we avoid taking any chances, trying new things, or taking all risks? Hasn't it been said that "with risk comes reward"?

The answer isn't to avoid all of the things that inspire the emotion of fear but rather to be clear with ourselves about what the real danger is. By asking ourselves, "What is the worst thing that could happen?" Oftentimes we realize the "worst thing" isn't really all that bad. In fact, many times the outcome of allowing our fears to rule us such that we do nothing creates a far more negative outcome. Franklin Delano Roosevelt, the 32nd president of the United States, is famous for having said,

"The only thing we have to fear is fear itself."

Do this: Every time you're faced with an uncertainty, presented with a new opportunity, or looking to make a change, ask yourself, "If I do this and it doesn't work out exactly the way I would like, how bad is it really going to be?" Get to know your unknowns. Are they really all that bad? Do you really need to be afraid of them?

Step 2: Take Away Your Downside Risk

In any endeavor we pursue in life there will always be inherent risks. As we sleep, we face the risk of rolling over and falling out of bed. As we walk, we face the risk of stubbing our toe and falling. When we're eating our lunch, we run the risk of biting our tongue. Nothing is without some degree of risk. However, oftentimes, there are simple things that we can do, small adjustments we can make, that can minimize these risks and greatly increase the likelihood that we will get the outcomes we desire.

MAKING SURE THE WORST DOESN'T HAPPEN

In 1957, *Fortune* magazine named J. Paul Getty, the richest living American. Getty was an oil wildcatter who had borrowed money from his father to buy land in Oklahoma. At the age of 23, he struck oil and his ride to riches began. Throughout his lifetime he amassed a multibillion-dollar fortune and collected millions of dollars in artwork and antiquities.

When asked about the secret to his success, Getty famously said,

"I always think about the worst possible things that could happen and then spend my time making sure they don't happen."

(continued)

> Strangely, most of us will do this in our day-to-day lives without giving it a whole lot of thought. We don't leave shoes hanging around where someone could trip over them. We wear seatbelts when we drive our car. We brush our teeth to ward off dental problems. We buy insurance to protect our valuables. There are a host of things we do every day to avoid problems down the road.
>
> Yet, when we are considering pursuing something more grandiose than brushing our teeth, we fret and worry a lot, but oftentimes don't make a list of the potential downside risks and the simple things we could do to avoid them.
>
> Following Getty's advice enables us to make our unknowns more known and develop meaningful strategies to minimize the possible bad outcomes. If this simple wisdom helped J. Paul Getty become a billionaire, what could it do for us?

Do this: What are the most important things you are working on right now? What are the biggest things you really want to accomplish? What ideas have you been thinking about but are afraid to pursue? Take the time to look at the worst possible things that could happen if you move forward. Then ask yourself what exactly could you do to minimize or eliminate those risks. (Hint: doing nothing, taking no action or avoiding all risks is absolutely the wrong answer.)

Step 3: Focus More on What You Want Than What You Don't Want

What we think about most often shapes our beliefs. Our beliefs are what guides our life. They define who we will become and what we will achieve.

People who rule their fears possess tremendous clarity on what they are looking to accomplish, and they think about it frequently. Visualizing what their life will look like, the things they will be able to do, and the opportunities that will open up to them. They know what they want and why they want it, so they willingly pay the dues to get it.

Conversely, people who are ruled by their fears have a lack of clarity on what they are trying to achieve and why it is important to them. They are focused on getting through the day rather than the bigger picture of the life they are trying to build. Because they have a limited vision, limited dreams, and limited goals, they aren't motivated by a higher sense of purpose. They see no clear benefit in pushing themselves outside of their comfort zones, so by default, they think about the worst possible outcomes. What happens if it doesn't work out? What hardships will befall them? The author Terry Litwiller once said,

"Success comes from having dreams that are bigger than your fears."

Do this: When you feel the rising apprehension of fear and uncertainty, ask yourself, what is your overriding purpose? What is it that you truly want to accomplish? What is it that means something to you? Once you've defined this, visualize what your life will look like once you've achieved it! How will you feel about yourself? How will accomplishing this affect your abilities in the future?

Thinking "Right" Activity

Remember, our dominant thoughts shape our beliefs, and our beliefs drive our actions. Here are three affirmations that will help you make this important transition. Repeat them often in your mind.

- *Fear is just my brain telling me I am outside my comfort zone.*
- *When I do the things I fear, my fears die, and I grow.*
- *My greatest successes and joys live on the other side of my fears.*

PEOPLE–LEADER PERSPECTIVE

Fear is a super emotion that leaders will battle against nearly every day. In many ways fear is like kryptonite to innovation, change, or the adoption of new strategies. It just stops people from taking action. The interesting thing is people will rarely admit they are afraid; rather, they will hide their fear behind excuses, rationalizations, or justifications as to why they can't do something.

Helping people recognize and acknowledge their fears is a healthy thing that leaders can do to assist people in becoming more comfortable with being uncomfortable. Oftentimes, sharing examples of times when you were afraid or uncertain and how you worked to overcome this debilitating emotion builds a humanizing bond with your people and helps them feel more comfortable acknowledging their own fears. Also, looking for ways to remind people of their *limitless ability to learn* plays a major role in assisting them in finding the courage to move forward in times of uncertainty.

PART 4

Finding Your Peace of Mind and Defining the Rebooted You

The highest order of life is finding peace of mind. It has been a central focal point of humankind since the dawning of civilization. In every early culture, the greatest thinkers of the day searched for the source of enlightenment, the pathway by which we could find inner peace.

We often think of our modern-day society as being the most advanced, the most intelligent, and the most highly skilled. Although we certainly are a marvel of technology, what frequently was sacrificed, lost, or discounted along the way was the wisdom and insights of many of those who have gone before us. However, more and more, as our ability to scientifically study and understand how our mind works, we are coming to realize that thousands of years ago, the greatest thinkers understood far more about what creates peace of mind than we perhaps realized.

CHAPTER 19

Finding Peace
in Your Time

A year ago, if someone had asked me where I thought I would be able to find peace of mind, likely my answer would have been, "Sitting on a mountaintop with the Dalai Lama in Tibet." Little did I know that it would be found with much less travel required.

In fact, it was David Vago who helped me home in on the illusive value I had chased my entire lifetime. David is a cognitive neuroscientist who earned his PhD about 10 miles from where I live. He was first introduced to me by Dan Harris (you remember him—Dan is the author of *Ten Percent Happier*).

David teaches at Harvard Medical School and does his research at Vanderbilt University. What he showed me is how to remold my brain and with it to find the one value that had eluded me for the better part of my life: peace of mind.

David taught me that our brain is made up of about 80+ billion neurons. Think of these like the branches of a tree; where they make contact with other branches, they can transmit information from one to another. Connecting these neuron branches is what are called *synapses*, which are like the telephone lines that transfer the signals from one branch to another. We have a lot of these synapse connection points in our brain (about 150 trillion of them).

Up until relatively recently, it was believed that once our brain was fully formed in adulthood, it largely stayed the same over the course of our lifetime. However, David and researchers like him have discovered that really isn't true. Today, we know that each of us has what is called activity-dependent plasticity in our brain.

Whoa, activity-dependent plasticity, did anyone else go into tilt mode reading that? I've got to admit, just thinking about that term gives me a little bit of a mental nosebleed. Okay, let's bring this ship back to earth for us non-neuroscientists. In very simple terms, activity-dependent plasticity means that our brain is constantly rewiring itself, creating new synapse connections between those neuron tree branches. Therefore, we can literally rewire our brain, shaping it in ways that bring us peace of mind.

Here is how David explained it to me. Our life is made up of a series of experiences or moments. David said we get 63,113,904 of these every single year. What we know of these moments comes to us through our five senses (sight, sound, smell, touch, and taste). Now, our brain will filter out a lot of these sensory inputs as being unimportant (remember, we talked about that—our reticular activating system does this for us); for the other ones it takes about 500 milliseconds for the MQ filtering mechanism of our brain to perceive and evaluate them. This is the time it takes for our belief system to make a determination whether a sensory input should be perceived as a threat to us or an opportunity for us. All of this happens at a subconscious level without our even being aware of it. In about another half a second we become consciously aware of these sensory inputs.

This is the most important part; catch this. If we slow down enough, stop, and reflect at this critical juncture we can consciously decide how we want to respond. Once we become consciously aware, we can actually override the instinctual nature of our subconscious mind right here in this moment in time. We can decide how we want to feel. We can decide, do we *want* to feel threatened, on guard, or at risk? We can decide if we want to get angry or remain in control. We can consciously decide if we want to be afraid or remind ourselves about our *limitless ability to learn* and adapt.

It turns out, slowing ourselves down mentally and making more conscious decisions about how we *want* to feel about the things that are happening has a rather remarkable impact on our brain. It literally rewires our brain. The circuits that we focus on more often become stronger, just like a muscle becomes stronger the more we exercise it. The more often we consciously decide to be calm and in control, the stronger this process in the brain becomes. The more often we decide to be patient and accepting, the stronger this circuit in our brain becomes. And the beautiful thing is, every year, we get about 63 million opportunities to practice strengthening the positive circuits of our mind.

However, this process doesn't just work this way for the more positive circuits of the brain; it also works the same way for the negative ones (fear, anger, resentment, anxiety, and so on). If we don't consciously practice looking for the opportunities and strengthening the positive circuits, the evolutionary wiring of our brain will automatically find the threats and reinforce the negative ones.

We've talked about how our brain is wired for survival through being hyperaware of perceived threats and risks. It will automatically default to more fear-driven negative responses. This is how evolution wired us; however, if left to its own devices this default, automatic response will never enable us to find peace of mind. It was never designed to; it was just designed to keep our ancestors alive millions of years ago. Today, we know we can consciously override the negative, threat-driven, fearful aspects of our mind.

How do we do this? Well, you've already been practicing it. We override the negative by reminding ourselves that we are *ultimately responsible* and have the *limitless ability to learn*. This helps us to see the opportunities instead of the threats. Doing this strengthens the calmer, rational, and more peaceful aspects of how our brain perceives our life. We are strengthening our mind just as we can strengthen our muscles. The process all comes down to how we consciously choose to use that critical half-second response time by deciding how we really want to feel versus just allowing the evolutionarily driven negativity of our subconscious mind to do it for us.

WHAT ARE YOU FEEDING?

Hundreds of years ago, the area where I live was inhabited by the Cherokee Indians. They were a tribal people who grew crops and hunted the lands for food. Their elders held the history, legends, and lessons from the past and handed them down through stories from one generation to the next. For thousands of years, this is how they lived.

(continued)

There is a wonderful Cherokee legend about life and the struggles we face within. It is a story of a conversation between a grandfather and his grandson.

One day, an elder is sitting fireside with his grandson. He looks at the young boy and says, "A fight is going on inside me. It is a terrible fight between two wolves. One wolf is evil—he is full of rage, anger, envy, arrogance, greed, fear, insecurity, lies, and laziness. The other wolf is good—he is filled with love, joy, peace, generosity, truth, empathy, courage, and faith. These wolves are both fighting for supremacy. I feel their battle in my heart every day."

"This same fight goes on inside the hearts of everyone, including you, my grandson."

The young boy reflects on these words and then looks to his grandfather and asks, "Which wolf wins?"

The wise elder looks into the young boy's eyes and says, "The one you feed."

More than 2,500 years ago, the Taoists spoke of the inherent yin and yang of life. For everything there is a balancing element. The Taoists felt that without this contrasting factor, nothing would exist, for there would be no referencing point. For summer there is winter. For man there is woman. For positive there is negative. For the day there is night. For good there is evil. You see this balanced symmetry in everything, even within us.

For sorrow we have joy, for happiness we have sadness, for anger we have peace, for envy we have contentment. Every day these emotions and many of their cousins will ripple through our minds, driven by chemical reactions occurring deep within our subconscious mind. For eons, it was thought by many that we were powerless against these emotions. They were created by the forces of evolution, and we were destined to be pawns to their omnipotent influence.

However, more and more we are coming to realize that within us we have far greater power than we once may have thought. We have the choice about what emotions we feed, what we focus on, and what we allow to consume us. We cannot eliminate the negative aspects of our life, nor would we want to. After all, you would never experience joy if you didn't know sorrow, you would never experience happiness if you didn't know sadness, you would never experience peace if you didn't know anger—the negative contrast creates our referencing points for all that is good. However, we now definitively know that we can consciously decide how much we want to empower these negative emotions.

We can feed whatever wolf we choose.

Find Peace in Your Time

In 2004 country music artist Tim McGraw released the song "Live Like You Were Dying." The song was based on his father, former major league baseball player Tug McGraw, who was diagnosed with inoperable brain cancer in 2003 and passed away in January 2004.

The opening verse of the song says:

> **I was in my early forties,**
> **With a lot of life before me,**
> **And a moment comes that stops you on a dime.**
> **I spent most of the next days, looking at**
> **the x-rays,**
> **Talking about the options,**
> **Talking about sweet time.**

In the chorus of the song, the dying father says to his son, *I hope someday you get the chance to live like you were dying.* It is a moving song that spent seven weeks as the #1 country song that year.

What is it about the prospect of dying that changes our perspective on time? Why do we need the finality of our life ending to begin to cherish our most precious thing—our time? Although these next questions may seem a little morbid, I'll ask you any way:

- How would your life change if you knew you had a week, a month, or a year to live?
- What would you do differently?
- What would you want to say to the people you care most about?
- What would you want to do as your days were winding down?
- What legacy would you want to leave?
- What difference would you like to make?

STANDING BY THE GRAVESIDE

When I was 23 years old, my father's father passed away. I hesitate to call him a grandfather because I really didn't know him or have any type of relationship with him.

(continued)

He was a difficult man. In many ways he seemed like an angry man who resented the way his life had turned out. I know nothing of his upbringing, dreams, or ambitions; I just know that he was gruff and seemed to drink a lot. I would see him at family functions, never smiling or engaging with people, just sulking off to the side.

When I answered the phone that afternoon, it was my aunt calling to tell us of his passing. My younger sister was standing in the kitchen nearby. As I hung up the phone, I shared the news with her. In the same instance, we looked at one another and both said, "No great loss to society."

That moment has always stood indelible in my mind (perhaps because it was likely the only time my sister and I have ever held the same thought). More likely, though, it is because it caused me to reflect on the fact that here was a man who walked the planet for 78 years and at his passing, even his family members felt it was "no great loss." What a waste.

We all have moments in our life that shape us, that define something in our mind, that cause us to see something powerful and important for us. That afternoon in the kitchen was one of mine. Why? Because in that moment I gained a measure of clarity on what I have come to believe is one of the truest measures of success.

For most of your life, everyone around you will try to define success, your success, for you. They will tell you it is a big house, a fancy European sports car, designer clothes, or exotic vacations. They will lead you to believe that money and prestige are the measure of success. They will spend millions (perhaps billions) of dollars each year trying to paint a picture for you of what your life should be, how it should look, and what you should have and do. While they will profess to be experts, in reality they know very little.

What I have come to believe is a truer measure of success is the difference we are able to make in the time we are here. What positive impact have we had? What lives have we changed for the better? Have we made this world a better place in some way?

We may not be the researcher who finds the cure for cancer or discovers a means of feeding the hungry. We may not have buildings named after us because we donated millions of dollars or funded the construction of a hospital. The difference we may make doesn't need to be grandiose or extravagant—and perhaps it is even more powerful if it isn't.

Ultimately, you have to decide what would you like people to say about you when you can no longer speak for yourself. What difference do you want to make? What ripple effect do you want your life to have? I would encourage you to ask these questions of yourself sooner rather than later, because more time is always better than less time, especially when it comes to making a difference.

Where Are You Living?

When initially asked this question, most people will inherently think of the name of the town or community they live in. However, there is a much more fundamental and important answer to this question. So let me ask again, "Where are you living?"

At the most fundamental level, each of us can only be living in one of three places: the past, the present, or the future. These are the only three places where our thoughts can live. You see, our thought process works very much like a single-channel, serial processor in a computer. It can't consciously be in two places at one moment in time.

Donald Hebb has been called the founding father of neuropsychology. Through his research in the 1940s, he discovered much of we know about how the brain's neuro networks communicate with one another and how our thought process works. Interestingly, one of the things he discovered was that our subconscious mind can process millions of simultaneous inputs, but our conscious thoughts can only be processed one at a time. (You can test me on this. Go back to the beginning of this paragraph and try to read and count at the same time—try it; I'll wait. Couldn't do it, could you?)

Now why is this important to understand? Well, think about it: because our conscious thoughts can be in only one place at any one moment, the only time we can be thinking about the past or the future is in the present moment. Any time our thoughts are living in our past or in our future, they absolutely cloud our ability to be focused in the present moment. Being lost in thought keeps us from finding the beauty of what is right in front of us, right now in the present.

The past, the future, and the present. All of these places can seem incredibly real in our mind, but, in truth, only one of them is actually 100% real and has any chance of actually being true.

Living in Our Thoughts of the Past

In the 1880s, German psychologist Hermann Ebbinghaus was one of the first researchers to begin to study the nature of our memory. What he discovered was our memory is nowhere nearly as accurate or complete as we may think. Ebbinghaus talked about what he called the *forgetting curve*, in which he showed that the accuracy of our memories erodes rapidly over time. (Ebbinghaus was also the first researcher to use the term, the *learning curve*, a little piece of trivia that may come in handy for you one day.)

Since that time, neuroscientists and cognitive psychologists have shown that not only do our memories fade over time but also we are constantly rewriting them. Basically, each time we recall something we shift the story slightly, adjusting our perceptions, the facts, and details, and then our brain rerecords the memory based on the most recent version we have told ourselves. So our memories are constantly evolving. The journalist Maria Ressa once said,

"A lie told a million times becomes a fact."

What we think are the facts in our mind are just the stories that we have retold, reshaped, and rerecorded a million times over.

And here's the wild part: likely our original memories weren't even all that accurate to begin with. We all perceive and interpret things differently; we have internal referencing points and perspectives that shape our initial memories. Stress, anxiety, and heightened emotional states also create a significant degradation in the accuracy of our memories. This is the reason why 78% of criminal cases that are overturned by the discovery of new DNA evidence had initial convictions influenced by eyewitness testimony. The stress and anxiety of witnessing a crime made people's eyewitness memory inaccurate.

The first challenge from spending too much time living with our past thoughts is our memories just aren't all that accurate. The second challenge relates back to our motivational intelligence. (Remember, it's our ability to manage negative thinking and self-limiting beliefs.) People who struggle with their MQ and who spend too much of their time ruminating on their past will have a significantly higher likelihood of suffering from depression. This is but one more reason why rebooting our MQ is so critical for our mental well-being.

Living in Our Thoughts of the Future

When we are living in our future, our imagination abounds. We are visualizing imaginary situations, creating stories, and projecting a pretend reality into our time ahead. So by its very definition, living in our future can't be real. At best, it's a guess at what we think is to come, nothing more than a somewhat random roll of the dice influenced by predictions.

Although mediums, psychics, and fortune-tellers who claim to be able to see into our future have captivated audiences for centuries, there remains very little evidence to support the accuracy of their claims. For the average person (i.e., you and I), our ability to see into the future isn't any more accurate than the charlatans who hustle people with tarot cards or crystal balls.

On the surface, daydreaming about our future doesn't seem like an altogether bad thing; after all, what's the harm in visualizing a brighter day or a better tomorrow? There really isn't one; however, what studies have shown is that most people aren't thinking happy, positive, rosy thoughts as they look into their future. No, quite the contrary. What most people are thinking about when their thoughts travel toward the future is worrying about what is going to happen down the road. The head of the University of Chicago Department of Psychology, Mihaly Csikszentmihalyi says that the default position of the brain is to worry. This is often where our thoughts of the future will land. People who struggle with negative thinking or self-limiting beliefs (low MQ) and whose thoughts lean toward the future are more prone to experiencing anxiety.

Living with Our Thoughts Focused on the Present

Being fully aware and engaged in the present moment is the only true measure of our reality. It's the only thing we have that offers us the slightest prayer of being real. **Stop!** Think about that point for a moment: the only real thing in your life is this exact moment *right now*. Anything else is just an inaccurate memory or a fantasy.

All of your life is happening right this moment.

Sadly, a Harvard study published in the *Journal of Science* found that for most of us, our thoughts tend to stray far more toward our past and future than they do focusing on our present moment. Our mind constantly wanders and spends a huge amount of time on self-reflective, negative thoughts and needless worrying, another vestige of our evolutionary journey driven by the singular goal of survival.

While at the Massachusetts Institute of Technology, German neuropsychologist Ernst Poppel studied extensively how the thoughts of the human brain constantly move from the past to the present and to the future. What he found is that our minds only linger in the present moment for about three seconds at a time before shifting to our memories of the past or our worries of the future. *Three seconds.* Three seconds of paying attention to the only real aspect of our life before we lose focus and get lost in thought again. How incredible is that!

The author Shannon Adler once said,

"The true definition of mental illness is when the majority of your time is spent in the past or future, but rarely living in the realism of the NOW."

The research shows we live far more in an illusory state than we realize, and in the process miss much of the beauty of our present life.

DISCOVERING YOUR PRESENT

Being truly present and in the moment can feel as elusive as finding Sasquatch or the Loch Ness Monster. It seems in our modern society there is always something fighting for our attention. We constantly bounce from thinking about the project we need to get done this weekend, to our upcoming trip, to the meeting that didn't go so well earlier in the day. Reflections, regrets, and worries about the future flow like an endless stream through our conscious thought process.

The only time researchers all agree that we are 100% present is at the moment of orgasm (a little gift from evolution to make sure we keep having babies). Although the prospect of living in a never-ending orgasmic state may seem like a promising way to be present, sadly, it is neither physically nor realistically possible. (Bummer, huh?) Yet the benefits for finding a way to live a more present life have been well documented by researchers over the last two decades:

- **Lower cortisol levels**—think of cortisol as your body's "alarm" hormone. It kicks your system into overdrive. Too much cortisol leads to anxiety,

---

depression, heart disease, memory lapses, sleep issues, and weight gain. Lower cortisol levels are a very good thing.

- **Decreased stress**—too much stress causes headaches, higher blood pressure and blood sugar levels, muscle tension, increased risks of heart attacks, and a compromised immune system. Less stress is always better than more stress if your goal is to live a long and healthy life. A Yale study showed that higher stress levels speed up our biological clock and shorten our life span.
- **Better sleep quality**—getting more rest sharpens our brain function and stabilizes our moods. It also gives our heart a chance to rest and lowers our blood pressure and blood sugar. Sleep also boosts our germ-fighting abilities by strengthening our immune system. A study conducted at Oxford University showed a lack of sleep increases mortality risk by 24%.
- **Better brain functions**—learning to live more in the present also boosts our creativity, increases our ability to focus, and lowers our mental reactivity.

Although likely we can all find some meaningful benefit for ourselves on this list (if you can't, you may want to admit to yourself that your standards are just too high), really being present just doesn't seem like something that comes easily for most of us.

So how can we gain the benefits of living more of our life in the one real moment we have—right now?

This is a question I posed to a number of cognitive psychologists, neuroscientists, Tibetan monks, mindfulness experts, yoga teachers (and pretty much anyone else who I suspected might have a valid insight). Here is what they told me:

- Consciously work to separate yourself from your devices; 5.3 billion people on the planet now have a mobile phone or connected device (that's 67.8% of the world population), and they will spend an average of three and a half hours a day looking at it. That will amount to about 8.74 years of their life staring at a screen. Add this to the time we spend in front of our tablets and laptops, and you quickly get a sense of our ever-increasing screen time. More and more, research is showing this not only detaches us from being present but also causes increased levels of depression and anxiety.
- Reconnect with yourself and your environment. Take the time to notice what is going on around you (this also helps us break out of the autopilot mode we discussed earlier). Look around and take in all that you see.

(*continued*)

Make special note of colors and textures. Ask yourself, "How am I feeling right now? How are my feelings influencing me?" Take a few deep breaths and slowly let them out. Dr. Andrew Weil taught me a powerful ancient pranayama technique that teaches 4–7–8 breathing (take a 4-second deep breath through your nose, hold it for 7 seconds, then release it over an 8-second outbreath through your mouth). This technique has been proven to calm your body and focus you on being present by activating your parasympathetic nervous system.

- Practice really connecting in conversations. Turn away from the computer or screen that is likely in front of you. Minimize any distractions and really look at the person you're interacting with. Give yourself permission to be mentally quiet and resist the temptation to start thinking about what you are going to say next in the conversation. Absorb yourself in their words without judging, evaluating, or critiquing. Just listen, really listen. At first, this might not be easy to do. Recognize that active listening and being fully engaged in a conversation is a skill set that is learned like any other: through practice, reflection, and refinement.

- Stop more frequently and just give yourself permission to hit the pause button. Take this time to think and reflect versus do and react. Reflection is one of the most underused activities, yet it provides some of the biggest rewards. Earlier we talked about the three most powerful self-reflection questions: What's working? What's not working? What can I do differently to be even more successful? Now would be the perfect time to use them.

Leveraging Your Golden Hour

When I was working with a client organization in Anchorage, Alaska, one of the women in the group was a nurse who had spent a portion of her career as a helicopter medivac specialist helping trauma patients quickly get hospital care. She explained to me that there is a term in the medical community called the *golden hour*. It's the critical 60 minutes after someone has been seriously injured. It's believed that getting proper medical attention within this window of time greatly increases the survivability of a life-threatening injury.

You and I also have a golden hour; it is the time each day when our mind is most impressionable and when we can have the biggest impact in rewiring it. However, it isn't one contiguous hour; it is actually two 30-minute segments of our day.

What researchers have found is in the 30 minutes after we awake in the morning and the 30 minutes before we go to sleep at night, our brain is in an alpha wave state. This is a time when we are most impressionable and thus have the greatest ability to rewire our brain. It is the best time to leverage the activity-dependent plasticity of our brain. (Sorry, I just couldn't resist using that term again.)

YOU DIDN'T BUILD YOUR CAR . . .

Twenty-five years ago, I remember watching my mentor, Joe, teach classes on self-leadership. He would stand in front of groups of people captivating them with insights, perspectives, and wisdom relating to how they could improve themselves and, in doing so, improve their life. Along with the group, I would watch him, learning from him both as a presenter and as a person.

One time, a woman in the group raised her hand and asked, "I didn't build my mind. How can I possibly learn to control it?" Joe pondered this question for a moment and replied, "Well, you didn't build your car either, but you learned to control it." At the time, I thought it was a simplistic and trite response, that in one regard rang true (I could in fact control my car); however, it didn't really help me in any way understand how to control my mind.

To me, my mind felt like a rodeo bronco, kicking and bucking, running, and racing in a million different directions, each seeming somewhat random. How could I possibly control such a beast? It just seemed far too untamed.

Then one day I was talking with Katy Thomas, who worked for our company at the time. She was young and yet had a wisdom that in some regards exceeded her years. In our conversation, she brought up the topic of meditation and how it had helped her to calm her restless mind. I listened and was intrigued but unconvinced it could help me. How could I possibly sit quietly and have my mind be calm and still? It just didn't seem possible. Yet the seed had been planted.

As the years passed, more and more of the people I met spoke to me about the benefits they had gained through meditation. I remained intrigued, and perhaps some of my resolve and wariness began to wane, but I still had no idea how or where to begin. Then Sean Johnson joined our company, and he talked to me about how companies were building smartphone apps to help people begin the practice of meditation. This gave me a sense of direction, a place to start.

(continued)

I remember one night I was in Baltimore, Maryland, and had a big seminar I had to deliver the next morning. As I lay in bed in my hotel room, my mind was racing thinking about the presentation, the things I wanted to share, and my desire not to forget anything important. As such, I just couldn't seem to settle down and get to sleep (never a good thing if you want to be sharp and focused for an important presentation).

So, I grabbed my iPhone and went looking for a meditation app. I downloaded one of the more highly rated ones that had a beginner's section for rookies like me. As I sat in my room, listening, following the directions, just trying to concentrate on my breath, an amazing thing happened—my mind quieted. What? Could there possibly be something to this meditation stuff? Could it really allow me to influence the direction of this mental bucking bronco?

It turns out, the answer was *yes*!

Prior to my reboot, I meditated sporadically at times when my mind seemed particularly agitated and hyperactive. However, after I returned from the hospital, I began to meditate more consistently every day. Here's how I use my golden hour.

Each morning as soon as I wake up, I take 20 minutes to meditate. I use two apps (10 minutes on each). I've found this makes an immense amount of difference in my days. I am calmer, less reactive, and more aware of thoughts and feelings as they arise. This gives me the ability to consciously decide how I want to respond as things come up in my mind. Do I want to allow something to upset me, frustrate me, or aggravate me? Or do I want to accept what is happening and respond in a more measured and productive way? I think this is exactly what David Vago and researchers like him have discovered about our ability to steer the way our brain wires itself up. We can develop trained optimism to overcome our evolutionarily engrained pessimism.

Candidly, the change in the way my mind works feels a little like a superpower. I have actually caught myself in times where I know I would have flown off the handle and yelled in the past, and now I just consciously let the negative thought flow through my mind without acting on it. Is it 100%? Am I perfect at doing this? No; however, I'm getting stronger at it with each passing day.

For the nightly half of my golden hour, I take the time after I lie down in bed to reflect on the things I am grateful for that happened that day. Similar to meditation, at first this seemed a little silly; however, with time it has made a great difference. I find that I don't take things for granted like I used to. I notice and appreciate more of the simple things in my life. As a side bonus, I have also found that I sleep better and almost never have bad dreams anymore. (I can't say for certain there is a correlation—however, these are both great things.)

Can I control my mind now? Perhaps Joe can control his; I'm not quite there yet. What I can control is what I pay attention to, what I empower in my mind. To me, this is good enough.

Time Expands

In November 1955, British naval historian, Cyril Northcote Parkinson published his most famous work in *The Economist* magazine. What he discussed ultimately came to be known as Parkinson's law. In the article, Parkinson made the observation that

> **"Work expands or contracts for the amount of time that we allot for it."**

Anyone who has ever been astonished by how incredibly productive they are on the day before they leave for vacation can attest to the validity of Parkinson's law. However, what Cyril Parkinson observed about the nature of time applies to much more than work. In fact, former Soviet president Mikhail Gorbachev once said,

> **"Parkinson's law works everywhere."**

Every aspect of our life will expand to fill our time, regardless of its relative level of importance. Time will escape us; there will never seem to be enough of it, until one day our time will be up, and we will have no more. If we don't consciously choose where we want to spend our time, things will always come up to fill it for us. Time slips away if we don't protect and steer it in those areas that will make the greatest difference.

Three Simple Steps to Gain Control of Your Most Important Time
- Make a decision regarding your golden hour. I shared how I use mine. These two 30-minute segments each day represent your greatest opportunity to invest in your peace of mind. It is an investment that

will pay far greater dividends than any stock or savings account. It is your investment in you, your happiness, your satisfaction, and your peace of mind. Everything else will hinge off of how you perceive your world.

• Make a decision about how you want to invest your time in your physical health each week. You don't need to run marathons or become a power lifter: just take more walks, drink more water, and get out in nature more. Each of these things will help you become more present and aware of what is happening in your head.

• Make a decision about how you want to use your time to improve your relationships and the lives of the people you most care about. Using our time to be more connected and provide benefit to others causes the release of three incredibly powerful chemicals in our brain: dopamine (which creates a sense of feel-good satisfaction), serotonin (which creates a sense of belonging and pride), and oxytocin (which makes us feel loved and trusted).

Thinking Right Activity

Here are two affirmations to help you develop the right thoughts about the value of your time. Repeat them often in your mind.

• *My time is my most valuable asset. If I don't protect it, it will get stolen away from me.*
• *The quality of how I use my time will define the quality of my life.*

PEOPLE–LEADER PERSPECTIVE

In every role in an organization (including yours as a leader) there are a multitude of different tasks and activities that have to be juggled every day. Not all of these are of equal importance. Yet oftentimes people will weigh these activities equally in their mind. When it feels like there is too much to do and everything is a perceived priority, the natural outcome is people feel overwhelmed and begin to think there is no way for them to succeed. What follows is disillusionment, disengagement, and, ultimately, employee turnover.

Your people will rarely feel like there is enough time in the day, and in many cases they will feel overwhelmed by the priorities and conflicted and

---

confused by what they view as shifting goals and unclear strategies. Unfortunately, these are the realities in many organizations. There is one simple thing you can do as a leader that will make a major difference.

Make a list of all the activities that a person on your team must execute on. Once you have the list compiled, rank these activities from least important to most important. To complete this aspect, consider the goals or metrics of the role, that is, how important is an activity related to achieving the goals. Activities that are critical to accomplishing to goals of the role should be ranked higher.

Next, take the top seven activities (the highest ranked or most important); these are the highest payoff activities (HPAs) of the role. In other words, these seven activities have the greatest impact on the success of someone in that given role.

Two of the most valuable things you can do as a leader are the following:

• Help your people to understand the HPAs of their role. Explain to them that when push comes to shove, focus on completing the HPAs first. With this, you have created a powerful way to help your people prioritize and manage their time.
• Coach your people to become proficient in completing each of their HPAs. By using HPAs as your framework for coaching, you are reinforcing the importance of the HPAs and demonstrating your commitment to helping your people to succeed.

Following this process will breed greater loyalty, commitment, and success on your team. It will also help you to become a highly effective leader.

CHAPTER 20

Finding Peace Through Love

The first known use of the word *love* only goes back about 800 years ago. However, virtually all cultures dating back to the ancient Greeks spoke of what we know today to be love. The Chinese, Japanese, Indian, and Persians cultures all have a version of love woven into their etymology. Love is also integral to every major religion. It seems that the concept of love has been with us as long as civilization (and likely even longer).

Why has love been so central to the rise of human beings? Perhaps it is because it represents the central force of goodness, positivity, and belonging. Love brings us, pulls us, together. It gives us support and strength to carry forward in times of difficulty. It rallies us to fight for a higher calling and makes us long for things that matter.

Love also seems to play a major role in the long-standing lore and stories handed down through the centuries. The central protagonists always seem to root back to good versus evil, love versus hate. Perhaps these two aspects resonate with us because we each feel the opposing forces of light and dark inside of us.

WHAT IS YOUR FORCE?

Years ago my mentor asked me if I had ever seen the movie *Star Wars*. Being a child of the 1970s, I don't think it would have been possible to have missed this iconic film.

He talked to me about the concept of "the force," the underlying source of power that both the good and evil characters drew from. He then asked me if I thought that the concept of a "force" was just mythical movie magic or something that might play out in each of our lives on a daily basis.

I considered the question and reflected on my own life and experiences before I answered. At the age of 25, I found myself thrust in front of groups of people, not because I had any desire to be a public speaker; candidly, the idea of that terrified me. However, the company I was working for was in a do-or-die position, and I had little choice if I wanted to do my part in helping the company survive.

At first I was terrible, awkward, uncomfortable, and stilted in my delivery. I'm quite sure that as painful as it was for me, it was even more painful for my audiences to watch. Perhaps they took pity in the pathetic wretch in front of them and stayed just because we are all drawn to watching a train wreck. Nevertheless, it gave me the opportunity to practice. Anything we practice enough, we eventually improve on, and this is what happened for me.

Slowly, groups became more engaged as I became more comfortable and dynamic. My self-consciousness waned and I learned how to draw a group in and carry their emotions. Admittedly, it was a little addictive for the shy, introverted, scared kid inside of me to watch people be captivated by my words.

It was at this time when I first felt what my mentor was referring to as the "force." It seemed like a power that I could wield to move people, get them to lean in, and influence their thoughts. I think I was too naive to consciously recognize how this new ability could be used for both good and evil.

So, reflecting back at my mentor's question about the existence of a "force" like power, I answered, "Yes, I do think that something like that exists."

He smiled as he looked at me. I think he knew that I had felt both the darkness and the light inside of me. He explained something I'll never forget. He said, "The most powerful people you will meet in your life will be the ones who knowingly draw their power from one side or the other. The more polarized they become, the more powerful they become."

Next, he used a simple analogy to help me to understand. He said, "Imagine it is like a roadway where on one side is the force of good. This is where love, acceptance, empathy, and selflessness live. On the other side of the road there is the force of evil. On this side of the road is where hatred, anger, jealousy, and greed live." He explained, "Most people walk down the center line of the road, sometimes drawing their power from one side or the other. However, because they live in the middle of the road, they never really gain the full power of either side."

He then looked at me and said, "You've spent your life in the middle of that road, but you've felt the power of both sides. I'd like you to pick a side, what team do you want to align with? Once you've decided, knowingly align with those values, draw your power from them, and watch what happens."

I made my choice that day. I picked the team I wanted to be on. I can't say I have always been perfect; I've made my mistakes and danced on the dark side. However, I quickly realized that wasn't where I wanted to live. I've seen people who lived there. They can seem incredibly successful and look like everything is perfect, but it's all an illusion. In relatively short order, their seemingly perfect existence comes crashing down and their world crumbles to dust.

Let me ask you, what side do you want to draw your power from? Make a conscious choice and watch what happens.

Greed Is Good

It was Gordon Gekko, the iconic character from the 1987 Oscar-winning movie *Wall Street* who said these words:

> **"Greed is good. It captures the essence of the evolutionary spirit. Greed, in all of its forms; greed for life, for money, for love, for knowledge has marked the upward surge of mankind."**

When that movie was released, I was a newly minted 24-year-old finance MBA, and these words were like a rallying cry for me back then. A beacon, or north star on which to guide one's life. Grab as much as you can of everything; therein you'll find your fulfillment, satisfaction, and peace of mind in life. I thought greed was the basis of what made everything great. It drove competition to be better and businesses to become more profitable. It was the foundation of a successful career and a life well lived.

However, as time went on, I began to understand the myopic nature of greed. Its singular focus on always achieving more frequently led to a selfish and self-centered perspective. Greed is exclusive and alienates others. Where one succeeds, another must succumb. Greed drives people away rather than pulling them closer. Greed begets hate, not love.

Albert Einstein once said,

"The three great negative forces in the world are greed, fear, and stupidity."

Where does greed live in our lives, how does it show up, how does it masquerade itself? Greed drives most of our risky yet unwise behaviors. It offers the illusion of comfort and distraction from our emotional baggage and traumas. Greed causes us to chase acquisitions versus more meaningful relationships. It fixates us on objects, things, and desires and causes us to look away from the best aspects of life.

Greed fuels addictions, overeating, obsessive behaviors, excessive spending, selfishness, narcissism, and a host of other undesirable traits. So why is greed so powerful? Why do we allow it to rule us if it leads to so many negative consequences? Greed is the siren song that plays to the darkness inside of us. It is as additive as heroin to our lesser self.

The antidote to greed is love, unselfish love. Love is the kryptonite to darkness; it is all that really matters in life. Love is the ultimate measure of success.

11/21/2022 AT 9:14 AM EST

As I sit here this morning with my coffee resting beside me, I'm reflecting on where I was one year ago today at this exact time. It was a dark hour, perhaps my darkest.

Five minutes before, I had been told by the doctor at the urgent care facility that my body was shutting itself down, and my cells, organs, and brain were starting to die. Nothing can really prepare you for a message like that. It's something you never think you'll hear someone say to you.

My first thought was of Michelle and the kids. Would I get the opportunity to watch their lives unfold, marriages, children, all that they would become? Would I even get to see them again?

I was tired, so tired. I felt like I was gasping for air, but it just wasn't there. Imagine holding your breath and then finally giving yourself permission to breathe and nothing is there. Oddly, I wasn't afraid of dying. Somehow, I knew whatever came next would be okay. I was sadder about all that I would miss—my family—I love them so much. This is what I was thinking as I rode in the ambulance that morning.

The next five days were a whirlwind of nurses and doctors checking me, shots, pills, IVs, tests, alarms ringing, and monitors beeping. A cacophony of activity and noise that disorients your senses and makes you feel like a spectator in your own life, with no control or understanding of what's happening and why.

Due to the care of a lot of great nurses and doctors, I was fortunate; I turned the corner. I got to come home whereas about 7 million other people didn't. It's sobering to think about that fact.

My recovery was long and slow. I felt a significant tightness in my chest, and my breathing was quite labored; the doctors explained that this was due to the significant scar tissue in my lungs. However, they assured me that my lungs would rejuvenate over time.

I also easily became disoriented and mentally overwhelmed. I had to pace myself and avoid too much mental stimulation. Even watching TV or listening to music made me feel mentally exhausted. It took months before I felt like it was safe for me to drive.

Today, my breathing has returned to normal, the pain in my lungs has largely subsided, and my strength has returned. The only lingering effect is a slightly diminished sense of taste and smell. All in all, I am well and feel so grateful for it.

It is amazing how much we can take for granted in life. The simple acts, things we just do every day—taking a deep breath, having the energy to walk, hugging your loved ones, laughing with friends—I take so much more pleasure in these things. I now know how quickly they can go away.

We are all busy, juggling far too many things, carrying worry and regret, experiencing the emotions of life. Our days tend to slip away far too quickly. This experience has taught me that the best aspects of our life often happen when we are busy being distracted by things that really don't matter.

Cherish and protect your time, use it in a way that makes a positive difference in your life and the lives of those around you. Look for ways to make the world a better place, the simple things, a smile and friendly hello, less judgment and more empathy, a willingness to be of service.

Most of all, let all those people who are important to you know how much you love them. You never know when you might not get another chance to do so.

The Givers . . .

In the early part of the 1900s there lived a man by the name of Andrew Carnegie. He was many things: a Scottish immigrant, a self-made man, a business tycoon, and great philanthropist.

His was a true rags-to-riches story. As a young boy he worked in a cotton factory making $1.20 per week. He went from there to working in a telegraph office and then to becoming a bond salesman raising money for American enterprises in Europe. All the while he frugally saved his money and made investments in railway sleeping cars, bridges, and oil derricks. Slowly these investments began to pay off and his prosperity grew. He foresaw the need for steel to fuel the expansion of railways and buildings, so he next invested in the steel industry. Ultimately he built what came to be known as Carnegie Steel into one of the largest steel producers in the latter part of the 1800s.

Carnegie spent the first two-thirds of his life working diligently, building a business empire. Through his endeavors he amassed his first great fortune. Then in 1901, he decided to sell his entire steel operation to the investment banker J. P. Morgan, which made Carnegie his second great fortune.

J. P. Morgan would go on to use Carnegie's steel company as the basis to create U.S. Steel, the largest steel producer in the world in the early part of the 1900s and, at one point, the largest corporation in the world. (U.S. Steel was also the first billion-dollar company in history.)

There Carnegie found himself, with a fortune worth about $300 billion (adjusted into today's dollars). Imagine being 66 years old and having so much money that if you laid the dollar bills end to end, they would wrap around the earth more than 1,200 times.

This is where Andrew Carnegie's life became truly interesting and worthwhile, because in the last 20 years of his life, he gave his fortune away. He became the world's first great philanthropist, endowing concert halls, museums, colleges, libraries, scientific research, education, and the pursuit of peace.

In his later years, Carnegie asked himself, "Why? Why was I able to amass this great fortune while so many other people struggle just to make enough to put food on the table and afford a roof over their head?" The more he pondered the question, the more he came to realize that all of his success could be attributed to a singular philosophy. A philosophy so powerful that it was literally the key to his great fortune.

What was this philosophy? It is called the Universal Law of Service. It simply states,

"The only way that you can ever truly get what you want in life is to first help other people to get what they want in life."

You can only *get* by *giving*—first.

People who are givers do so willingly, without reservation. They give of their time, their energy, and their appreciation for what others around them do. They are people who are thankful and grateful when others reach out to help them and they actively look for ways to repay the favors or good deeds that others do. People who are givers understand the value of love and they work to multiply it.

. . . And the Takers

There are two types of people you will meet in life: takers and givers. Takers live by the all-too-familiar motto of "What's in it for me?"

They go into every situation, every opportunity asking themselves, What am I going to gain by doing this? How am I going to benefit? What's in it for me? Theirs is a self-centered perspective that gives little thought or concern to others; in essence, they feel that their own personal well-being should always take precedence.

The takers' "what's in it for me" philosophy is the antithesis, the polar opposite, of the law of service.

The takers are always looking for an edge and how they can get something out of someone; their greed fuels them. They feel entitled, deserving, and even, in some cases, worthy of having others do for them. Why? Because they think they're smarter, more clever and cunning than others, or in their mind they are less fortunate, unlucky, and passed over.

Many times the takers in life believe successful people had their success handed to them, things given to them, and all of the lucky breaks and circumstances conspired to create a more perfect world just for these successful people. The takers in life have bought into all those limiting myths you've long since let go of.

As the takers sat back and watched other people's lives become better and better, and their lives got worse and worse, they couldn't help but begin thinking, "Why shouldn't these more fortunate people give some of their good fortune to me?" So they held out their hands and waited. Remember, victim thinkers never win.

What the takers in life fail to recognize is that success in every area of our lives is always driven by a better mindset, a more optimal perspective (the mindset and perspective you have developed with your newly rebooted brain). Remember, takers have bought into the myths and mistruths. They fail to recognize that these myths are nothing more than a set of shackles that bind them to a life of unhappiness, mistrust, and dissatisfaction. Takers will never find peace of mind; it's just impossible.

All the while the takers had failed to notice that those who had worked hard and were more ambitious were really doing almost all of the giving. The givers were using their more optimal mindset and perspective to pursue calculated risks, learn from their mistakes, and create opportunities. In some cases, this led to starting companies and giving jobs to people. The givers were donating money to help people who were truly disadvantaged to live better lives. They were giving their time to help lift people up and assist them in becoming self-sufficient. The givers were paying taxes to build roads, fund schools, and create police and fire departments.

Look around you: everything of magnitude, everything that has stood the test of time was created because someone was a giver, not a taker.

So if you've been waiting for someone or something to give you your big break, to hand you the opportunity of a lifetime, or to whisk you away from your suffering—*stop waiting*!

Stop waiting for someone to give you something. Stop holding your hand out. Stop waiting for someone else to tell you they care about you. You make the first step. Give first. Givers get; takers get taken from.

The only way you can get what you want is by helping others to get what they want—first.

LIFT WITH LOVE

I was recently in St. Petersburg, Florida, working with a client group. One member of the group, Cassandra, comes into the room in the morning with a big smile on her face and proudly announces to the group that she had already accomplished her goal for the day.

Curious, I ask her, "What was your goal?"

She explained that every day she sets a goal to do five positive things for complete strangers. This may be saying "hello" or "good morning" as she walks down the street. It might be letting someone in front of her in line or as traffic is merging. It may be taking an extra moment to sincerely thank someone or tell them how much she appreciated that they just made her that cup of coffee or served her at a restaurant.

Certainly it is easy to become self-absorbed, focusing on our own busy schedules, the things we must get done, and how quickly the time in our day is dwindling. However, I remember sitting there that morning and thinking about what a profound effect this simple act of human kindness could have. It doesn't have to be grand, time-consuming, or in any way diminish what we need to get done, yet it is a simple way that we can make a positive difference every day.

Perhaps our actions will inspire another person to be a bit friendlier, to smile instead of frown, to see goodness in a difficult time or to be reminded that everything isn't all bad. Five simple positive things a day.

I decided that morning, I too was going to adopt Cassandra's goal. I was going to work each day to pay it forward, to give to others, to share more love than I take. I hope you will too.

Three Simple Steps to Spread Love

1. Make a list of the people who have had the greatest positive impact on your life. Think back to your childhood, teen years, and early adulthood. Look at those influential people in both your career and in your personal life. We've all had those special people who've made a difference in our life. Add them to your list. Once you have your list compiled, systematically begin to reach out to the people on it. Don't overwhelm yourself and try to get to everyone in the next day or week. Just pick one or two people a week. Reach out to them and let them know how much they have meant to you, share with them the difference they've made in your life, thank them for what they did. This is a powerful way to share appreciation and love.

2. Set aside some time to sit down with the people you are closest to. Have a conversation with them about their goals and aspirations. Find out what's most important to them and ask how you can help them to achieve or accomplish these things. Make what's important to them important to you. Then each week, focus on doing things to help the people you care most about.

3. Make a conscious effort each day to be a more positive force. Take a moment in an otherwise dull elevator ride to say "good morning" or "hello" to someone. Smile at that person passing you as you walk down the street. Open a door for a someone you don't know. Compliment someone or make them laugh. Tell someone how much you appreciate something they have done for you. Find those simple ways that you can make the world a slightly better place.

Thinking Right Activity

Here are two affirmations to help you develop the right thoughts about spreading love. Repeat them often in your mind.

- *In every decision I make, and in every action I take, I can spread more love or more hate. I'm choosing to spread love.*
- *The only way I can ever get what I want is by first helping others to get what they want.*

PEOPLE–LEADER PERSPECTIVE

Do you know the goals and aspirations of each member of your team? Not what they company expects of them, but what they would like to accomplish for themselves. What is it that they would like to learn? What would they like to achieve? What do they see as the next step in their career? What would they like to focus on or be involved in?

Remember, the only way to get what you want is by helping others to get what they want. The most powerful leaders understand and leverage the law of service to lift their team. Understanding the wants and needs of their people enables great leaders to foster higher levels of engagement, commitment, and loyalty.

Make what is important to your people important to you, and you will be amazed at what a difference it will make in your team.

CHAPTER 21

Redefining
the Rebooted You

We, as human beings, only find happiness when we are in pursuit of something that gives us a sense of growth and fulfillment.

The great Greek philosopher Aristotle wrote these words to his son, Nicomachus, more than 2,000 years ago. Through our journey together you have removed the shackles that bind so many. You have realigned your belief sets back to where they belong, where they were on the day that you were born. You have learned tools to keep yourself properly rooted in the right mindset. You have rebooted yourself, and with that a new and better world awaits you.

With your newly rebooted brain and the perspective it creates, you've given yourself the opportunity to move through life unencumbered. You have regained your ability to become. The question now is, what will you do with your newfound freedom? How will you leverage the rebooted you? Where will you find your sense of growth and fulfillment? Who and what do you want to become?

DEVELOPING YOUR COMPLETE GAME

Years back I was running a client meeting and I met a man by the name of Dan Pultney. He left an indelible impression on me for many reasons; however, the first thing that struck me about him was the fact that he stood six-foot, ten-inches tall. You typically don't meet too many people in your life who have to duck down every time they walk through a standard-sized doorway just to keep from breaking their nose.

Because he was so tall, I asked Dan if he had grown up playing basketball.

He said, "I played all through high school and even got a scholarship to play basketball in college. My dream was to play professional basketball in the NBA. Unfortunately, I had a knee injury in college that changed my plans."

Later Dan was talking to me about his son. So, I asked if his son had inherited Dan's genetics; was he tall as well?

Dan said, "My son is 15 and already six-foot, seven-inches tall. I think he will end up every bit as tall as I am, maybe even taller."

"What about your love of the game of basketball? Does your son have that as well?" I asked.

"Absolutely; he wants to get a scholarship and play for Duke University. It is an amazing thing to watch, it could be a driving snowstorm outside and my son will shovel off a portion of the driveway and be outside shooting baskets at 10 o'clock at night. You literally have to drag him back into the house some nights," he said.

"Wow, that it a pretty impressive work ethic for a 15-year-old kid. You must be very proud," I replied.

"It is, and, yes, I am very proud of him, but unfortunately he's not going to get a scholarship to play at Duke or anywhere else for that matter," Dan said.

I looked at him quizzically. "How can you say that? You just told me he has the work ethic, he's practicing, he has the height—why wouldn't he get a scholarship?"

I will never forget Dan's reply.

He said, "The challenge is, my son only practices the aspects of the game that he likes. What he doesn't do is practice the aspects of the game that he doesn't like. As a result, he has developed a very incomplete game. No coach is going to recruit him because he doesn't have a complete game."

I remember standing there a little stunned because I had never thought about this idea of a "complete game" before. Later that afternoon, I was back at my hotel and I was reflecting on what Dan had shared that morning. As I was thinking about it, something hit me like a ton of bricks. What I realized was that this idea of a complete game went far beyond just the game of basketball; it applies to virtually everything in life.

Earlier in our conversation, we talked about how most lottery millionaires end up filing for personal bankruptcy. Why does this happen? Well, think about it. They haven't developed their complete game for building a strong financial life. Here they have this huge check, but don't know how to invest and protect their newfound wealth. All they really know how to do is spend it, so that's what they do. Their incomplete game causes them to lose all their lottery winnings.

So, there is a complete game for building a strong financial life. There is a complete game for building great relationships. There is a complete game for maintaining good health. There is a complete game for everything of merit in our life.

Amazingly, the complete game in each of these areas of life doesn't differ from one person to the next. The fundamentals of what enables a person to create financial stability (saving, investing, minimizing personal debt, and so on) are exactly the same for everyone. We may not all be starting from exactly the same place (you may have more saved than I do, someone else may have more debt, and so on) but the fundamentals of the complete financial game are exactly the same for all of us.

The same can be said about the complete game of physical health: eating right, exercising more, stretching our muscles and improving our flexibility, getting enough water and sleep—these things benefit every one of us. Each of these is all part of the complete game of physical health.

What about relationships? Is the complete game of building great relationships the same for all of us? Let's see. Do we all need to respect our partner's values? Do we all need to understand and support one another's goals? Do we all need to be proactive communicators and good listeners? Do we all need to be able to forgive (and really mean it)? Yup, we do. I guess this complete game is universal here as well.

So there is a complete game for everything of merit that we do in our life and that complete game is exactly the same for every one of us. Wow, that was a major eye opener for me.

Once this realization hit me, I couldn't help but begin to ask myself, "Dave, where have you developed your complete game?" In my finances, I could think of a few things I did well and other things that I really didn't pay much attention to—incomplete game. In my physical health, I worked out, I got some aerobic exercise, then it hit me: I hate to stretch—incomplete game. Earnestly, prior to my reboot, I struggle to think of a single area of my life where I could say I had a complete game.

(continued)

I quickly came to a rather startling realization, I was doing the exact same thing as that 15-year-old kid. I was focusing on the things I liked to do and shying away from other things—even though those other things were really important.

I've come to realize this is true for most people. They practice the things that come easiest for them. They invest their time in things that they can do quickly so they can get on to the next thing. Most people never develop a complete game in any area of their life. Thus, they never accomplish all that they are capable of.

There is just no exception: *before you can have, you must become.* Becoming means developing your complete game, focusing on all of the aspects required, not just the easy ones. If you and I want to "have" in life, we must "become" in life. We just have to keep reminding ourselves—with our rebooted brain, we can become whatever we *want* to become. Your rebooted brain and the perspective it is built on enables you to develop your complete game in every area of life. Stop and think about how few people understand what you understand. Think about what a blessing that awareness is.

If You Don't Define Yourself, Others Will Try To

Look all around you. Watch the commercials that run on TV and the internet. Look at the ads that run in magazines and online. Listen to the words that come out of the mouths of the people in your life, relatives, friends, teachers, employers, and peers.

As you do this, one undeniable theme begins to come clear—everybody is trying to tell you who you are and who you should be. They are trying to define you, to tell you what you are capable of and what you are not. Recognize that not everyone has your best interests at heart. Many people will advise you on who you should become, not necessarily because they want you to be more, to be better, and to be happy or fulfilled. Rather, they do it because it serves their needs. It makes them feel better about themselves to hold you back or because it helps them sell products to make them more money.

By defining you, they get to define themselves. However, what gives them the right to shape who you are? Why should they have the power to influence your feelings, your beliefs, and your confidence level? Why are their words and their thoughts any more important than your own?

Ultimately there is only one person who is capable, who truly is worthy of defining you. That awesome responsibility lies solely in your hands. You must decide who you are. You must decide where you want to go. You must decide what you want to become. Your rebooted brain gives you the ability to define or redefine every aspect of your life.

Sometimes the Simplest Decisions Can Make All the Difference

"Simplicity is the ultimate sophistication."

Leonardo da Vinci stated these words more than 600 years ago. Later, Apple cofounder Steve Jobs would use them as the fundamental ethos of a company that would change many aspects of our world. Simplicity is the purest form of greatest.

As human beings we tend to complicate things. We seem to almost innately say to ourselves, "That seems too simple. It can't possibly work that way." Or at least, "It can't possibly work that way for me."

Defining yourself, shaping your life, moving yourself in a better, happier, and more fulfilling direction is no more difficult, no more complicated, than making the conscious decision to arrive at work at a certain time. It just comes down to asking yourself a few simple questions.

As you answer the following questions, I want to caution you. *Do not* answer these questions based on who you were yesterday. Answer these questions based on who you want to become tomorrow. Who you are today doesn't really matter; who you want to become is far more important. Leo Tolstoy, one of the greatest writers ever, once said,

"What matters is not the place we occupy but the direction we choose."

Defining Your Path

First, take a few minutes and define a path. This doesn't have to be your "be all and end all" path. Your path may fork and take a different direction as you journey forward; that's okay. Just the fact that you are on a consciously defined path and leveraging your rebooted mind makes all the difference.

You don't have to plan out the next 10 years of your life. Just look into the future for the next 12 months. Where would you like to see your life a year from now? Take out a notepad and ask yourself these questions:

- What would you like your career to look like 12 months from today? What would you like to be achieving or accomplishing in your work life? Make a list of a few things that would make you happy to have accomplished in this area of your life. Remember, work is your financing vehicle; it is how you earn the resources to build the rest of your life. How do you want to maximize this opportunity? Write down your thoughts.
- What would you like the financial area of your life to look like 12 months from today? Our finances (or lack thereof) are one of the major areas of stress and pressure for most people. Wrestling control of this area of your life makes a huge difference. So, what would you like to see happen in your finances over the next year? Are there some debts you would like to pay off or pay down? Would you like to have a certain amount of money in savings or investments? Make a list of a few things that would make you happy to have accomplished in this area of your life. Write down your thoughts.
- What would you like to see happen in your personal relationships over the next year? Do you want to find a partner or make a new friend (or would you like to get rid of one)? Is there someone who you've lost contact with who you would like to reconnect with? Would you like to do something, travel somewhere, or share an experience with someone you care about? What would make you happy in this area of your life? So much of the quality of our life is defined by the quality of our relationships. What would you like this area of your life to look like? Make a list of a few things that would make you happy to have accomplished in this area of your life. Write down your thoughts.
- What would you like your physical health to look like over the course of the next year? Sadly, our physical health often gets overlooked until it becomes a problem. We take it for granted until it no longer exists. (I can firsthand attest to this fact.) Let's not make that mistake moving

forward. What exactly would you like to see happen with regard to your physical health over the course of the next year? Write down your thoughts.

- Last but not least, what else would you like to see happen in your life over the next year? Is there a hobby or interest you would like to pursue? Are there some projects you would like to get done? Is there someone who needs your help or support that you have been considering reaching out to? Think about your life as a whole; is there anything else you would like to see happen over the next 12 months? Write down your thoughts.

There you have it. That wasn't so difficult, was it? Just five simple questions to reflect on. Be proud of what you've done—the journey you have followed and all that you have accomplished through your reboot. Be proud of the fact that you have defined a path, a better path for your life moving forward. Most people never take the time to think about the path they want to follow. They just let life and their broken brains take them where it may, sadly, and all too often this just leads to unhappiness and despair. Author and CEO Hendrith Vanlon Smith once said,

"An unplanned day invites both distraction and destruction."

But this is not your path. You know better, you believe better, and your rebooted brain enables you to live a life most can only hope for, wish for, and dream of.

Defining Your Person

Now that you have clarity on where you want to go and what you want to achieve, it's time to think about who you want to become. On your notepad, answer the following questions. I encourage you to write out your answers (example: I am a _____ person.). Just the simple act of committing something to writing increases the level of importance it carries in your brain.

Here are some questions to help you to decide who you want to become. Which do you want to be?

- Someone who is a good person or a bad person
- Someone who is a happy person or a sad person
- Someone who is a positive person or a negative person
- Someone who is in control or someone who allows other people to take control
- Someone who quits or someone who persists
- Someone who makes excuses or who takes ownership
- Someone who allows their fears to stop them or someone who might be afraid but moves forward anyway
- Someone who is open-minded or close-minded
- Someone who tries new things or wants to stick with the way they've always done things
- Someone who allows other people tell them who they are or someone who defines for themselves who they are
- Someone who expects the best outcome or someone who expects the worst outcome
- Someone who takes risks or someone who plays it safe
- Someone who dreams big or someone who focuses on just getting through the day

Rest assured, you have the power, the ability, the intelligence, the character, and the fortitude to choose the path you want to follow and the person you want to become. You just have to consciously decide which of the choices you want yourself to become. Once you've decided, work on moving this way today. Practice being this type of person. Remember, what you practice most often you will become over time; it is all cumulative.

GREAT ADVICE, POORLY EXECUTED

It was three weeks before I was scheduled to graduate from college. The school had invited a speaker to come in and share some advice with us students as we embarked on the next phase of our life journey.

She was an engaging speaker who told compelling stories and had us laughing and reflecting on our journey ahead. The central theme of her message was about developing a plan for your life rather than just allowing life to take you where it may.

Her message resonated with me largely because I had always been a dreamer but not much of a planner. I could paint a vivid picture of what I wanted my life to look like; however, I had absolutely no idea how I was going to make it happen.

I remember one of the topics that she talked about was the importance of writing down your goals and aspirations. I thought this was a good idea and a great place for me to start. So after the meeting, I went home, pulled out a yellow legal pad, and began to feverishly write down where I wanted to go, what I wanted to achieve, and how I wanted my life to look.

Once everything was down on paper, I looked it over and smiled as I reviewed it. It was a comprehensive picture of my dreams and aspirations. Then I opened up my desk drawer and slid that notepad inside.

A year went by, then another and another. One day, I decided to clean out my desk (which is a good thing to do every three or four years or so). As I was throwing away papers, old bills, and the odd junk that accumulates over time, I came upon that old faded legal pad.

I couldn't help but once again smile as I reviewed all of the things I had written down all those years before. Then something hit me. Not a single thing that I had written down had come to fruition, not one. I couldn't help but ask myself, Why? Why had I failed so miserably in my attempts to pursue these things? Had I just set unrealistic goals? Were my time frames unrealistic? Had my life goals changed?

No, none of these things rang true. The truth was that I had written all these things down as a college student, stuck them in a drawer, and largely forgotten about them. It was as if once I closed that desk drawer as a college student, I just magically thought all those things would happen just because I had written them down. I had never focused on them, reflected on how I was doing, or adjusted my plans for achieving them. I just didn't take any actions to make them happen. Basically, I realized that consistent focus was the key.

So I decided to repeat the exercise, but this time not leave my list to collect dust in my desk drawer. I adjusted the list, revised my direction, and really thought about what I wanted my life to look like. Once I had put together my list, I got in the habit of looking at it every Sunday night.

With my goals in mind, I would build my weekly to-do list. However, I wouldn't just include the projects and things I needed to get done that week. I would also ask myself, "What's one thing I can do this week to get me a step closer to the life I want to lead?" Then I would also include this step on my to-do list. I found this made my weekly activities grow beyond just the day-to-day stuff as I began to focus more on my big picture.

At the end of the next year, I was again reviewing my life goals, and I had actually accomplished a number of things on the list. Others were a bit further off, but I could clearly see I was making progress on them.

Focus and Consistency Are Your Friends

Once you have made the decision of where you want to go (your path) and who you want to become (your person), you have to reinforce that decision each and every day. In 1826, French politician Jean Anthelme Brillat-Savarin wrote an essay in which he stated, "You are what you eat."

Although what we eat certainly has a bearing on our health and well-being, a more accurate statement might well be, "Your beliefs are formed by what you think about most often. You are what you give yourself permission to be."

Remember, your thoughts lead your mind. They can lead you in any direction, forwards or backwards. If your thoughts are leaning toward the negative, and this isn't where you want to go or who you want to be, actively work to let go of these limiting affirmations. When these negative thoughts creep in (and they will; they do for everyone), consciously force them out with positive thoughts of where you want to go and who you want to be today and tomorrow.

Realize that every day, with every thought we have, with every action we take, we are building momentum. Remember, everything in life is cumulative. Rarely does one thought or one action matter; however, cumulatively things matter a great deal. So be aware that each day you focus on doing positive things, you are building positive momentum. Build enough positive momentum and things begin to change dramatically.

You have the power to choose your thoughts. Exercise this power well and it will lead you exactly where you want to go. Your rebooted brain gives you this ability.

CHOOSE TO BE A GRATEFUL PERSON

Michelle and I were heading to the health club to get some exercise on an early Saturday morning. It was a crisp December day here in western New York, but the sun was shining and there was a little frost still on the ground. Within the first three minutes of being in the car together, she delightedly commented on the bright blue sky, the wild turkeys that were lingering in the field beside the road, and how excited she was about the day ahead. I couldn't help but get caught up in her sense of gratitude and enthusiasm.

As I marveled at her perspective, I realized how easy it is to lose sight of the simple joys of life, the wonderful things that are going on all around us. It is easy to take things for granted. It seems so easy to notice the bad stuff, the negative headline, the latest crisis, or the problem that just arose. Our brain naturally tunes into these issues. Sometimes (perhaps far more often that just sometimes), we just need to stop and really appreciate all that we have rather than all that we lack.

You're reading these words right now because you woke up this morning; be grateful for that. Likely, you have fresh water to drink and food to eat; be grateful for that as well. You can take a deep breath and smile; be grateful for that. There is goodness all around; you just have to slow down and look for it. Take the time to notice it; it's there, don't ignore it, embrace it, be grateful for it.

Recently I was listening to meditation guru Joseph Goldstein talk about the simple pleasures in life. He spoke of that first stretch when you get out of bed in the morning or step into a warm shower. The refreshing sense of a cold glass of water on a hot day or that deep belly laugh you get when someone says something really funny. He talked about looking up and feeling the warm sun on your face or watching the unbridled exuberance of children at play. Joseph talked about how every day we are immersed in these wonderous moments and yet so many go unnoticed and unappreciated.

If we stop and really pay attention, there is so much to be grateful for. Even simple little acts like brushing our teeth can be moments of gratitude. Each day we go through the act of brushing our teeth. It's a couple-minute chore that we routinely do. However, have you ever really slowed down and enjoyed the experience instead of just rushing through it so you could get on with your day? Try it. If you're home right now, go in and slowly brush your teeth, take your time, and really relish the experience. I'll wait.

Pretty awesome, wasn't it? It's like a little spa day for your mouth. A few minute, mini-mouth massage that you get every day for free. Think about the thousands of times you've brushed your teeth and really missed that great experience. But you'll never miss it again; be grateful.

Most of all, be grateful for the people you have in your life. The people who you love and care for. Be grateful for the time you get with them, the smiles you share, and the memories you've created together. Be grateful for what they've given you and what you can give back to them.

Earlier in our conversation, I mentioned that on Sunday, November 21, 2021, Michelle walked me to the door of the urgent care clinic and saved my life. As I reflect, I've realized that she has saved me in many ways; for that I am grateful.

A Final Thought

I have spent the better part of three decades traveling around the world, meeting people, and learning their stories. What I have come to realize is that many of those people will spend most of their lifetime waiting, wishing, longing, hoping that somehow, something, somewhere will change in their life and allow them to escape from the baggage of their past and build the life they want for their future. I spent 56 years of my life being this person. Wishing, hoping, and waiting for happiness and peace of mind to find me—all that found me was frustration, unhappiness, and depression. I believe this is why the poet Henry David Thoreau made the observation that "the mass of (people) live lives of quiet desperation."

However, you and I now recognize that we don't have to follow this well-worn path. We have been given a gift, an insight that enables us to know there is a better path, a happier path, a more peaceful path. We understand that we can escape the past and reboot our future. We have all the tools and knowledge we need.

The author Marianne Williamson once said,

Our deepest fear is not that we are inadequate. Our deepest fear is that we are powerful beyond measure. It is our light, not our darkness that frightens us most. We ask ourselves, who am I to be brilliant, gorgeous, talented, and fabulous? Actually, who are you not to be? . . .

We are all meant to shine, as children do. . . . As we let our own light shine, we unconsciously give other people permission to do the same. As we are liberated from our own fear, our presence automatically liberates others.

Within you there is a light and there is greatness. You may not have always seen this or believed in it, but my hope is you see it today and every day from this one forth. You have within you everything you need to master your fears, overcome your doubts, and conquer your demons. You have within you the courage to move forward even when you are afraid. With your rebooted mind, you have within you everything you need, and no one can ever take that away from you.

Always remember, I believe in you.

Rebooting Your Beliefs and Perspective Affirmation Plan

Use these affirmations to reinforce your rebooted awareness. The more you repeat these affirmations to yourself, the faster they will become the optimal dominants thoughts that will reshape your beliefs. (Remember, your beliefs will drive your actions and define your life.)

- I am ultimately responsible for what I choose to pay attention to and for the actions I choose to take.
- I have the limitless ability to learn.
- The more I practice, the better I perform.
- Permission to try and persistence in practice are what my success is built on.
- I am becoming the right person to take advantage of my right place and time.
- Circumstances don't control my destiny; I do.
- When I focus on doing minimums, I get minimums.
- Who am I going to be today, my maximum self or my minimum self?
- The harder I work, the luckier I get.

- With focus, perseverance, and an open mind, I can manufacture my own luck.
- Each setback makes me stronger, smarter, and one step closer to success.
- There are no unrealistic goals, just unrealistic time frames.
- Every setback teaches me how to succeed as long as I allow it to.
- The only true failure is to never try or to quit trying.
- Every day, I win or I learn.
- Feedback is the breakfast of champions.
- Feedback is my friend because it helps me learn and makes me better.
- Every day I seek feedback, it fuels my success.
- Fear is just my brain telling me I am outside my comfort zone.
- When I do the things I fear, my fears die, and I grow.
- My greatest successes and joys live on the other side of my fears.
- My time is my most valuable asset. If I don't protect it, it will get stolen away from me.
- The quality of how I use my time will define the quality of my life.
- In every decision I make, and in every action I take, I can spread more love or more hate. I'm choosing to spread love.
- The only way I can ever get what I want is by first helping others to get what they want.

Rebooting Your Life Action Plan

Here is your sequential plan for maximizing your rebooted brain and building the life you most desire.

Step 1: Define Your Direction (Revisit This Part Quarterly)

A. Make a list of the most important areas of your life (example, relationships, health, finances, career, and so on). Pick the areas of your life that you are most looking to succeed in right now. Once you have the list completed, prioritize it, making the most important area number one on your list.

B. Success always starts with one simple decision. What is it that you truly want to accomplish? Your answer doesn't have to be grandiose. Just pick something, anything, and truly commit to making it happen. Looking at each of the areas you listed, define one goal that you would like to accomplish in that area of your life. (You can add additional goals down the road; for now, just focus on one goal per area of life.)

C. Take each of the goals you defined and break them down into the smallest pieces possible. Although it may seem overwhelming to have a hundred little micro-goals, it is actually much better mentally to accomplish these small steps. It is a powerful way of showing your brain forward progress and keeping you on track.

Step 2: Build Your Plan (Repeat This Part Monthly)

A. With your micro-goals defined, now ask yourself, which of these do I want to accomplish this month? (Setting a shorter-term picture helps build our belief system and keeps you on track.)

B. What specific steps can you take each week to move your life in the right direction? (Don't be fazed if some of these steps don't work out. Remember, fail frequently. It is better to try something, have it not work out, and then learn from it than to do nothing and learn nothing.)

Step 3: Become the Person Who Can Make Your Life the Way You Want It to Be (Ongoing)

A. Who do you want to work on becoming this month? Make a list of the skills and abilities you want to learn or know you need to get better at.

B. Ask yourself: What would doing your very best at this skill or ability look like? What attitude would you approach it with? What would you seek to learn? What outcome would you most like to achieve?

C. Do you know someone who is better at this skill or ability than you are? Ask them to mentor you.

D. Where can you go to learn more about this skill or ability? (Google online courses, look for YouTube videos, check out Amazon, your local bookstore, or library for resources where you can learn more, and so on)

E. Define the ways you can practice this skill or ability.

F. Set up a practice/learning schedule (be realistic; start with 10 minutes a day).

G. Create a challenge or goal to help you map your progress. Don't be overly aggressive; be realistic, such as where would you like to be in two weeks?

Step 4: Remove Areas of Resistance (Ongoing)

A. Choose an area in your life where you are struggling right now. Take a few minutes and reflect on your circumstances in this area of your life. What aspects are positive or getting better? Where do things feel like they are stalled out or getting worse? Take out a piece of paper and make a list of these two areas.

B. Next, considering where you feel like you are stalled out or sliding backwards. Ask yourself these questions:
   i. What specific actions can I take to make forward progress?
   ii. What do I need to improve on in this area?
   iii. How can I practice this?
   iv. What are three things I can do today and this week that will make my circumstances better in this area?

C. In those areas where you are stalled out, actively work to seek out more feedback. The faster you can gather meaningful feedback in these areas, the quicker you will see improvements. (Remember, more feedback is always better than less feedback, so look for it in the areas of your life where you feel stalled. Ask for it if it isn't offered. Don't run from feedback; feast on it.)

Step 5: Build Your Support System and Creating Motivational Accountability (Ongoing)

A. Pick an accountability buddy, someone who is a positive force in your life and who wants the very best for you. Share your goals and plans with this person. Let them know the deadlines you have set and ask for their help in holding you accountable to them. It is amazing how much of a difference this small step can make.

B. Next, begin working to create a mastermind group. Pick a group of people who are looking to accomplish something in their life (they don't all need to be looking to accomplish the same thing; they just need to be positive, forward-thinking individuals). Bring these people together and share with them your idea of creating a mastermind group to help one another move forward in life. Set a regular time to meet. In each meeting, have each person share their forward progress and setbacks. Provide thoughts to one another regarding the lesson contained within the setbacks. Last but not least, at the end of each session, have every member set a goal or objective that they want to have accomplished by the next mastermind meeting.

Step 6: Minimize Your Risks and Fears (Ongoing)

A. Consider the most important things you are working on right now and the biggest things you really want to accomplish. Make a list of the ideas have you been thinking about but afraid to pursue.

B. Take the time to look at the worst possible things that could happen if you move forward. Then ask yourself: What exactly could you do to minimize or eliminate those risks? (Hint: doing nothing, taking no action, or avoiding all risks is absolutely the wrong answer.)

C. When faced with an uncertainty, presented with a new opportunity, or looking to make a change, ask yourself, "If I do this and it doesn't work out exactly the way I would like, how bad is it really going to be?" Get to know your unknowns. Are they really all that bad? Do you really need to be afraid of them?

D. When you feel the rising apprehension of fear and uncertainty, remind yourself of your overriding purpose and the benefits you are seeking to gain. Think about what is it that you truly want to accomplish and why it is important to you. Visualize what your life will look like once you've achieved it. How will accomplishing this make you feel about yourself? How will accomplishing this affect your abilities in the future? (Shift your focus to what you want to achieve. Let this consume you. Don't waste time and energy focusing on what scares you.)

Important Questions to Consistently Ask Yourself

Ask yourself: What important aspect of my life am I working on right now? Am I taking enough action in this area of my life (or am I spending too much time pondering, hoping, and waiting for something good to happen)? What actions can I take today to begin to build more momentum?

Ask yourself: What's not working here? Why isn't it working? (Hint: many problems aren't externally driven. How are you complicit in your struggles? Is there an attitude or a thought process that is holding you back? What are you avoiding doing?)

Ask yourself: Who are the people in my life who are most supportive of the direction I want to move in? Who are my naysayers and negative people? Actively work to spend more time with your supporters and protect yourself from the negative influence of the naysayers.

Ask yourself: Who are the people in my world who could potential help me? (It doesn't matter if they aren't your best friend or a close acquaintance; most people would be honored to help you if you just ask for their advice and guidance. Look for mentors and advisors; don't let your fears keep you from making these critical connections.)

Ask yourself: (Do this at least twice per day.)

- What's working? What am I doing right, right now?
- What's not working? What am I doing wrong right now? What have I been avoiding doing?
- What am I learning? What adjustments can I make? How can I do it better moving forward?

Ask yourself: What am I failing at right now? (If your answer to that question is, I'm not failing at anything, you're either lying to yourself or not trying hard enough. Face facts, we are all struggling with something, somewhere in our life. Some aspect of your life isn't quite where you want it to be. Don't pretend it is all right; own up to it. You can't fix something unless you first admit to yourself it isn't working.)

Next, ask yourself: What is it that I am doing (or not doing) that is contributing to my struggles in this area? (This is an incredibly insightful question, so be honest with yourself. Frequently, we are our own worst enemy and we don't even realize it. Based on the insights you gain from this question, fail forward by identifying specific things you can learn or do to make things better.)

Common Mistakes to Avoid

Don't do this: Don't get discouraged when things seem chaotic and unclear in the beginning. Success is always ugly in its early stages. With time, reflection, and refinement, the seemingly unorganized chaos begins to take shape and the pathway to success becomes clearer. Be patient and embrace this early ugly phase of success.

Don't do this: Don't listen to the legions of pseudo experts and false prophets telling you that you can't do it. (The world is full of people who would like nothing better that to include you in their club of mediocrity. If you want to be successful, if you want to be happy, if you want to realize your dreams and ambitions, you cannot follow the same pathway that mediocre people follow.)

Rebooting Your Peace of Mind Plan

Leverage your time to find peace of mind with these steps:

1. Make a decision and commit to how you want to use your golden hour. These two 30-minute segments (when you first wake up and just before you go to sleep) represent your greatest opportunity to invest in your peace of mind. It is your investment in you, your happiness, your satisfaction, and leads to your peace of mind. Everything else will hinge off of how you perceive your world. (Recommendation: meditate in the morning; reflect on what you are grateful for in the evening.)
2. Make a decision about how you want to invest your time in your physical health each week. (You don't need to run marathons or become a power lifter, just take more walks, drink more water, and get out in nature more. Each of these things will help you become more present and aware of what is happening in your head.)
3. Make a decision about how you want to use your time to improve your relationships and the lives of the people you most care about.

(Using your time to be more connected and provide benefit to others causes the release of three incredibly powerful chemicals in our brain: dopamine, which creates a sense of feel-good satisfaction; serotonin, which creates a sense of belonging and pride; and oxytocin, which makes us feel loved and trusted.)

4. Practice being more present by turning off your mental autopilot mode. Make it a point to notice new things when you are driving (find five unique or different things each time you get into the car to go somewhere). Practice this same exercise when you are walking, shopping, or doing things in your day-to-day life. Make it a point to mentally slow down and just notice things. (The first step in living in the present is recognizing when we aren't there. Turning of our mental autopilot forces us to "not be lost in thought.")

5. Next, begin to notice how your actions/behaviors connect. We all have behaviors patterns; spend time noticing yours. Where are these patterns leading you (in the right or wrong direction)? (The first step in breaking a negative behavior pattern is to notice it exists.)

6. Last but certainly not least, make it a daily habit to pause occasionally and ask yourself, "How am I feeling right now?" Next, ask, "Why am I feeling this way?" (Getting in the habit of recognizing your emotions and the drivers of them is an important step in making meaningful changes in your life.)

Leveraging Love to Find Peace of Mind

Leverage your love to find peace of mind with these steps:

1. Sit down with the most important people in your life (your spouse, partner, or significant other; your children; your closest friends, and so on) and ask them about their goals or aspirations. Take the time to discover the things that are most important to your most important people. Once you understand what these important people in your life are looking to accomplish, take the time to help them in these areas. Each week, focus on doing things to help the people you care most about. Make what is important to them important to you.

(Remember, the only way to get what you want is by helping others get what they want.)

2. Make a list of the people who have had the greatest positive impact on your life. Think back to your childhood, teen years, and early adulthood. Look at those influential people in your career and in your personal life. Once you have your list compiled, systematically begin to reach out to the people on it. Don't overwhelm yourself and try to get to everyone in the next day or week; just pick one or two people a week. Reach out to them and let them know how much they have meant to you, share with them the difference they've made in your life, thank them for what they did. (This is a powerful way to share appreciation and love.)

3. Make a conscious effort each day to be a more positive force. Take a moment in an otherwise dull elevator ride to say "good morning" or "hello" to someone. Smile at that person passing you as you walk down the street. Open a door for a someone you don't know. Compliment someone or make them laugh. Tell someone how much you appreciate something they have done for you. (Find those simple ways that you can make the world a slightly better place.)

ACKNOWLEDGMENTS

There are many people who have helped me in both my journey through life and in the process of what ultimately came to be in this book. Without them I would not have had the wisdom, confidence, experience, or courage to write these words and hopefully be able to help others with them.

I want to thank my parents who had my back as I was growing into adulthood and, as such, gave me the confidence to pursue my dreams while lessening the fear and consequences of potentially falling on my face. Mom and Dad, my life would have taken a dramatically different course without your example and support; thank you.

I want to thank my wife, Michelle. We have journeyed together since we were teenagers. Navigating life's triumphs and sorrows, its trials and tribulations, we have grown together and grown stronger. In so many ways, you are the person I aspire to be. Your kindness, empathy, and compassion are beyond measure. Without you, it is hard to imagine where my life would have taken me.

I want to thank my mentor, Joe Gianni. Like a marriage, our relationship hasn't always been an easy one. Yet you have stayed with me and helped me to see myself, my beliefs, my decisions, and my world from a fundamentally better perspective. Our conversations over the years have always lingered in my mind and helped me to unlock the parts of me that have held me back. I thank you for your patience, persistence, and wisdom. I am glad I asked you to be my mentor all those years ago in that Holiday Inn down in Rhode Island.

I want to thank our team at 2logical. I am honored to have each of you as part of my extended family. Sharing this magnificent career journey with you has been an incredible privilege. Your talent, perseverance, and belief never cease to amaze me.

I would also like to thank my friend Dave Smolski for both his encouragement and his introduction to the team at Wiley. Without your faith and persistence in helping me find the right publisher and editorial team, the words in this book would have only lived within my mind.

Last but not least, I want to thank all of those people who encouraged me to share my story and who helped contribute to this book. Many of you I have met throughout my journey; your stories, experiences, research, and insights helped to expand mine. Without you, this book never would have come into existence.

ABOUT THE AUTHOR

For three decades, David Naylor has been internationally recognized as a thought leader in the field of leadership development and sales consulting. Through his role as executive vice president of global learning and development for 2logical, he has become a trusted advisor and strategic consultant to scores of CEOs and executive leadership teams in many of the most recognized corporations around the world.

Through the years, David has been directly responsible for the design and implementation of countless successful leadership, sales, customer service, and productivity improvement training programs. American Express, AXA Financial, General Electric, Time Warner, BlueCross BlueShield, Charles Schwab, Pfizer, E★TRADE, Berkshire Hathaway, Eli Lilly, Bank of America, Procter & Gamble, eBay, Citibank, HSBC Bank, Lincoln Financial, Merrill Lynch, Viacom, and many other organizations all leverage David's leadership expertise.

David's company, 2logical, has developed leaders in more than 95 countries and is consistently ranked as one of the top 20 global leadership development firms.

David's Current and Past Board and Advisory Positions
- Advisory board member to social media company, LinkedIn.
- Advisor to United States Government–Small Business Administration
- Advisor to the State of New York
- Chairman of the board of business advisors, Rochester Institute of Technology, Rochester, New York
- Dean's council and advisory board member to Saunders School of Business at Rochester Institute of Technology

David Is a Contributor to These Magazines

- *Harvard Business Review*
- *Chief Learning Officer Magazine*
- *Forbes*
- *Inc. Magazine*
- *Fortune*
- *Fast Company*
- *Entrepreneur*
- *Training Magazine*

David's Awards and Recognitions

- Harvard, Distinguished Leader Award
- Forbes Leadership Council
- Training Industry, Top 20 Global Leadership Development Company

INDEX